LISTEN

LISTEN

Poems

Chan Kwan Ee Tom

atmosphere press

Table Of Contents

I

Starving. Hysterical. Naked.

Do not

go

gentle

into

that

g

o

o

d

n

i

g

h

t

.

LISTEN

I hear no voices in the streets, no midnight screeches, no nightmare
　　child frightened by unwanted ghosts in the night,
no homeless loitering, no tempered drunkards passing drivel by insomniac
　　bars, no Heineken bottles abandoned in sullen street corners,
no bobbing heads missing in drugged alleys, no spilled-over buckets
　　over amputated chairs;
no whispers left unaccounted for, no tight-lipped murmurs, no demurral
　　too bold to speak at will those loud primary colours: the blue, the
　　yellow, the menacing red that had once reflected on a cloudless moon
　　on bituminous roads—
no bloody clumps spilled like Campbell's tomato soup,
no fortresses assembled from traffic cones and cardboard boxes,
no arch stone avenues, no shelter for tears in summer's rain,
no paper pinwheels, no give-away lunches to be collected for free;
no child suffered *too* much, no child collapsed from duralumin leaks,
no gloaming silver sparrows soaring across the imminent skyscraper skies:
the city sweepers at night held their sighs,
their exasperations distilled in congruent minds scattered in the wind,
dragged on by the soles of their feet and had no place to go;
the living deck too small to move about escaping its timbering walls,
the damp peeling wallpaper too thin to keep our troubled minds at bay.
The city has no place for lucid dreamers
for there are no stars to look up to;
no quiet privacy living under scorching light,
no faith in hoping that someone is watching over us—
There are no angels in the city,
only innocent children who let themselves roam free in the darkness.

Dreaming

out of the trough:

Admiral port, Victoria,

vinyl on skip, static replay

one sunset boulevard

gazing up pride rock

haven

To listen and dream of a temporal hereafter of otherworldly expansion—
    with voices raised and spoke of pride with pride,
of undulating thoughts announced in high spirits to recount by date
    and number
the assembly of men, women and children out in the streets
to shout, vote and appoint a stage for public discussions,
to be heard in unison—the boys and girls who led the way
still wearing their learner shoes who spoke of a future in years to come,
a world they realised that can be ideally true.
You have heard them sing songs of hope, of grand ideals, of one in spirit
    to shape the hearts of men and women—the men and women who
    witnessed history being made in the span of months and years of
    finding from one contract to another;
who stand on unsteady feet in quest for knowledge, of identity formed
    in time to decide and germinate,
who take the virgin step and pull down the walls of bootstrapped quarantine
    and speak to neighbours they've never spoken to before,
who clamp their bodies—our bodies—together, turning inward, amassing
    for a time-honoured embrace for new life beginnings,
who raise their glass and meet you with sincere eyes,
who call you out by name—however you wish to be called—and say,
    "Hey! Good morning, and in case I don't see ya, good afternoon,
    good evening and good night!"

These few seconds of happy salutations are all it takes to lift your heart and
     lay down the strain you have endured in the game we called "Life";
to drop a few tears for you and me,
our shoes contain the residual warmth of company that no frayed or
     worn or tattered spirits would be roughened by faulty pavements
     of rubble and stone;
where in wintry smog we find in us an abode—
the mechanical city, though pigeonholed,
is a hegemonic place for love and sentimentality.
Where conscious historians bear the scourge of humanity to record the
     pigments of cordial history unbigoted on the fence
and flagpole monuments soar at the rendezvous point of love in vivid
     memories not forgotten but passed on;
the frightened newborn feeds on the tube and breathes the clean-
     conditioned air in the Bright Box smelling of fresh, green, smelly
     Earth;
tendril hands reaching out for support to feel the unmistakable gravity
     that is most certainly settled on land, not at sea;
and the graves at rest, remembered and respected,
their names live on in the ancestral plains
on south-facing mountains of wind and water where they made their
     residence;
a family-tree legacy runs in the veins and the alliance of blood moves
     your body to resist the never-ending fall
to stay afloat in the swirling cyclone that surrounds you and also the
     one growing inside of you.

Wander
off and around
commuting distant shores
an unbridled tribulation
of endless libraries
one unlikely
wakening

Those who are leaving or have already left—the British getaway migrating
    like a flock of Dodo birds—dream of hope elsewhere but never
    found.
Whispers gone rogue, the young with sensitive hands not meant to take
    up manual work eager to drop the condemning shovel,
much like their concerned parents who willingly smelt their lifelong
    earnings to forge the silver spoon for levelled chance
and bestowed upon them their dreams so they may live on prosperous
    and free,
that they may never need to break bread on the dinner table.
The promise of stability is enough to convince them to cast aside their
    parental bond:
enough talk of missing you, enough sopping tears, enough cruel words
    of love and attachment not amounting to anything… Cut the Cord.
    Send them away.
A one-way ticket to the land beyond of Timbits, Cadburys and Cherry
    Ripes,
a Neverland to retain their childhood innocence—how much will you
    sacrifice for love?
If only they had known… For what separates the masters and ladies
    from the diamonds in the rough is simply it:
only the moneyed persons are allowed to dream—the cream of the crop,
    the yellowest of corn—who would never need to serve or starve
    or punch buttons on the cashier to pay for rent or tuition;
and the ordinary, young schoolboys and girls are too ashamed to admit
the inevitable grip of the shovel and their calluses which grew for family
    pride.
There are those who seek refuge, who took to themselves the responsibilities
    of adulthood
with extraordinary passions and the vivid imagination of teenage dreams;
whose noble purpose fell short for that one fatal time and had to flee

for doing 'whatever it takes' and whatever it takes has taken them
    to commit to solemn vows and clip their wings in exchange for
    asylum:
Change your name! Change your identity! Abandon city! Abandon
    the camps of the blue and yellow divide! Abandon all!
For change has always been about moving forward and not dwelling
    in the past,
and look how they've drawn a few wrinkles on their faces—whether
    it is for the city, for the country or for themselves—they are burdened
    by the weight of newfound love;
Then there are those who follow fit, a centipede of bodies tugging onto
    one severed arm to another, brooding an ungoverned panic,
who never understood well enough if they were even prepared to depart
    the matrimonial city and to live like nomads, always on the move;
who coalesce in the way of the sheep and trudge on from one city to
    another in comfortable clusters,
who are never able to fit in to the local populous: had it ever crossed
    their minds as they graze upon their neighbours' grass and claim
    unequivocal right to live life as they should—they say, 'whatever
    it takes' in the name of survival—such is the nature of the social
    animal.
As short and limited a mind as a frog in a well,
domesticated men and women are too ingrained for cultural inclusivity;
by leaving the well, they move the well with them.
But who's to say that those who had never been brave enough to speak
    would ever speak up again?

Live on
blind Suara!
Gift of goodwill nightmares
To see the que sera, sera
split from the swallow's nest
the match rekindled
again

Our memories await for the daily preening, to start our morning routine
and pick through the scuff and muck, and from it, a string of cause-
and-effect from beginning to end:
to walk along the narrow street to work, bumping shoulders and limbs,
head down on telephone screens wondering how we've gone back to
the way it used to be.
Our efforts undone, the years of progress a myth we tell our children that
happily-ever-after only happens in dreams—but like all dreams, they
sometimes bleed into reality;
that somehow we see in the blurry downcast of the night, the yellow
raincoats and the boulevard of umbrellas gathered clear on for miles
on end like the wheat fields of Pienza—to touch the tuft with your
fingertips, or be touched by it, the persistent tufts that bloom more
abundantly than the flowers in July;
in passing fields the children chased on, reeling in the string that is attached
to their waist—the runner's kite half-visible in the clouds drifting
in unreachable distance:
"You'll get there soon enough," your parents said, the reason that kept
you staring at the sky at night, and they carried you on their shoulders
just to let you get a bit closer, a trip to the stars, and be the first child
on the moon with a rose for company:
a sensitive rose that is sensitive to time
and time again we knew that colours won't last.
Where in that burst of life how we've come to know that some moments
live on for an eternity if truly lived, of shared memories both bitter
and sweet—
that when the buds begin to bloom, how we pile our bodies around
it to build a fortress and a moat dividing all the evils of the world
from the loam of sacred ground;
how we brace ourselves against the harsh easterly winds and all forces
of nature they brought together with them to have you down on
your knees:

make way for the high-risers that will commence in no time!
The moor turned battlefield for Love and lover's beliefs,
there is no place for stubborn weeds in the five-year plan—
the mortars will level our bodies in holey ground:
Who could breathe through the layers of concrete in our wake?
So tread through carefully, pinch your heart and grab onto whatever
    green stems out from the pavement;
Should you find colour, assemble what's left of the flower in your chest;
for we knew that life would never be the same—but how we've tried!
How we've lived on most honest and true, and true is our spirits
to fend off all unholy sounds that haunt us in our every wake.
For our mad hearts beat on as a testament for love
and no changing of the name or longing distances would make us any
    less.
For we know our love for the city is genuine, and in eudaimonia we
    don't need to question how much it takes to break a conscious and
    well-functioning mind.
That when night falls and darkness resumes, the resounding shadows
    that persist to linger at the back of your ear: the whimpering,
    whispering, howling, rustling, squeaking, skulking, dripping, kicking,
    knocking, beating and rattling of harrowing nightmares, of bereaving
    flashbacks, of unlikely hopes and silence at heart that may never
    come—
Listen to all the voices that we've gathered along the way
for we have never seen anything as grand as this:
the inconsequential dreams
from one of many young, unsounding and lovingly displaced states of
    mind.

TREMBLING FEET

Trembling feet
ten feet off the ground
staring down the foul gutters
some unfortunate rat
splat when first encounter
the fallen head from the sky
split into two.

The caged bird
climbs the iron-barred fence
only to find
a decisive fall
reduced to a number
on an excel form.

The eye watches from the other eye
a new-found silence
piecing together
fancy pictures from the TV screen—
Beware the glassy skies!

The bodiless body resting cold
curdled blood
in a plastic bucket on the floor.

Roaming white shirts
badgeless uniforms
in disguise
the yellow umbrella tainted red

bloodied fists
red terror in the streets

Counting corpses
deafened ears
morbid eyes
withdrew silent tears.

The threat
an uneasy child makes
when walking
on trembling feet.

MOCKINGBIRD

I have never seen a bird that flew
so close to the ground
trailing behind
the swirling white smoke
descending
screams
                reaping
tender lungs
            with smouldering heat
      impetuous young
                clenching
tracheal collars
                choking
fabricated dreams.

The artificial fog blinds the vision.
Livid epiphora
        perpetuates   the sting,
then comes
        the hissing in my ear
the muffled gun
shoots
one lucky hit
            far across—
I feel it on my back
the scoring blade
        against   my skin;
        falling down

                    however
          not me
but the young man in black
          chasing tears

               I take the walk of shame
up the scissor stairs 2 am at night
hearing loud debauchery racketing next door
as the young scholar reads from the heat
and the generosity of their peephole light;
rediscovered history found,
not in books,
but the fish eye on the wall
that stands between the half-sized bed
and the cheating couples fucking on the other side.

Daybreak
I hear children talking
about the red bricks in the sky,
the shopping malls turned battlegrounds,
the black and white into newspaper red,
the mob and uniform bickering gunpower plot,
careful parents too afraid to talk—

Hush now, little baby, don't say a word.
Back to sleep, back to school.
Back to walking in your little leather shoes.

Because Daddy has a votive to give you the world:
a brass ring to mend a lifetime of malaise.
The fatal score plays on in the dead of night:
When have we ever stopped dreaming?

And I have never heard a bird that sings

so close

to the heart.

AWAKE

I

It is 2:00 at night when the alley dog starts to bark:
the first may be an accident, the second
responds for fun, the third follows the fourth
yapping all giddily, disturbing sleep.
Potty-trained collars jangle in submissive release,
more dogs join in on couch cushions of unlit apartments
barking for the sake of barking—*who goes there?*
The vagrant mongrel howls
at the waning phase of the moon,
who outbreeds the inbred shingles
and tantalised teeth—*where is your master?*
A feral call scorches the sky; others joined in,
stretched out their primal necks from terraces above
and disgorged an outcry enough to wake the entire city—
Remember who you are!
Remember where you came from!

2:15, a blinding light shoots from the ground,
an audible ultimatum to any wild thing
who dares cross the line.
A sharp whimpering
sends others running off to their burrows.
The streets resume its silent order
and the dark makes the bloody signs unclear.

The human child back to sleep
and you wonder:
where have all the dogs gone?

II

Follow the short artery
of unmanned motorcycles,
a low tail   shifting
through
dark puddles
dipping orifices
without reflection.
Turn away
and stand
          in the light.
Ignore
the whining baby
shrinking
in a greasy pizza box,
waiting
to be delivered to _____________

III

The abandoned shoe has no address. Like the crossing
of an unsupposed sentence not meant to exist.
Untied laces exposing worn-out tongue
pushed inwards around loose collar.
A side quarter peeling off, squashed
like a shrivelled discoloured prune.
Hollow eyelets enlarged after years of friction,
weathering and torn, toe cap bent 180 degrees up,
down and folded, capsized like an offshore boat.
A detached sole lay separate in the way of the route—
an *objet trouvé* as a chew toy for the young,
undisguised (Duchamp would be proud);
its size tells of an adult's foot
shoved in mud, hauls the mind
to think nothing of it and all of it: the helm,
to which holds the potential cup of water
in its damp chamber, inquires
you to paint a picture
you cannot avoid
and you pick your medicine
to quench your thirst,
returning, yet again;
you might as well own it.

IV

Like the sunfish, it keeps on swimming
sideways. Its lateral eye stalks for
plankton, sculling
to whichever direction
it is beckoned to go,
drifting and floating
in the vast salt water,
basking sun.
Its dorsal fins protrude
as if a shark's, yet
none so vicious
in all its white docility;
its kilo-stuffed belly
overturns,
exposed
prone to die
in over-sensitive ways:

To get dazzled by the morning sun, and dies.
To get stressed by an impending collision with a turtle, and dies.
To get shocked by salty seawater stinging its skin, and dies.
To get stressed by a bubble in its eye, and dies.
To get shocked by a nearby sunfish dying, and dies.
To get stressed by seeing a nearby sunfish being stressed, and dies.
To breach the water for a remarkably nimble krill, misses, and hits the water
    surface, and dies.
To mistake a plastic bag for a jellyfish, and gets it stuck in its throat, and dies.

So you take an angry bite
at its gall,
and munch on larger
chunks of the flesh
until
it dissolves
into a milky cloud
of clairvoyance
after rain
because
you know
it wouldn't scream

much.

V

Howling again, the dogs return
in the final hours of night.
Waning shadows,
the mongrel emerges
from beneath the soiling earth:
dragging
an unresponsive leg
in the middle of the open road
and settles down.
        Landing sideways
on its raw bony ribs,
        its blunt tail withdraws.
A lamentable lick   to recount
the odd number of knuckles
that make up for missing toes.

                    You wonder
where it is looking
and *what* it is looking for, and how
it would feel to read once more:
the final moments of flower balconies
lining overhead   and sympathetic eyes
whose shampooed hair and quiff
sticking out in view
to stand watch from a safe distance;
their round-collared necks
guarantee a lifetime of bliss
and pampered love—

they do not need to know
the way of the Pariah,
and the mongrel knows
it is not their fight to win.

So let it sink into anagoge,
oh misfortuned one!
Let blow flies patch your rotting wounds.
Let it come swiftly, in jaded time,
the blinding headlights will clear the path.
And once your chest opens up
like a rose, spewing life,
the howls will not end
for the rest of the night.

MAN

Give him a baton
so he may take arms.

Give him a badge
so he may act with official orders.

Give him a name
so he may listen and will obey.

Give him a voice
so he may read your every word.

Give him permission
so he may act out and justify his actions.

Give him indulgence
and you make him the freest person in the world.

Give him a backing
a mountain that he can lean on
and you make him the most powerful free-person in the world.

But give him freedom
and you will take his life and freedom away.

TRICKLING WATERS

Trickling waters
dripping down cold crevices
   into potholes
      on the ground.

Dreams engraved
on the half-covered sky
peering through
    a light
captured between   the spaces:
   paper-thin holes
a cross-generational infestation
   in cemented bricks
      leaking gold.

Tightened collars
strapped around the neck
made of copper not silver
   a life's choice
     served on civil tongue.
The papillary ridges on the walls
made too thin for the rain;
   two buckets filled
a third readied
in waiting   hands.

I placed
the upside-down watch
on my wrist
          as time follows
the clockwork
I put
in reverse

Counting backwards
to a non-existent number
written in sympathetic ink
thirty years ago:
5 35
a forboding memory
          began
once upon a time.

Absent tears fall
          like trickling waters
the white tile overshines
a new obsession
          of an unready child
turning over a deistic side of the coin.

The decaying walls
          unsurfaced
                    as loyal rebels
rummaged through
          history books
with cut-out tongues
and heavy heads
forced on tyrannical ground.

TO MY STUDENTS

1. ON WRITING SHORT STORIES

Talk about writing stories
reduced in lines
kept within two pages, a story
about a setting: place and time. Talk about

once upon a time,
one day, one Frabjous day
when little girl ventures into miracle lands
meeting mystical creatures beyond imagination:
the manxome, mimsy, callooh! Callay!
Down goes the Jabberwocky,
a gentle girl coming of age with hookah's advice.
Listen to Absolem—
whose riveting rhymes dribble
through enchanted streams;
children chasing dreams
about a setting: place and time. Talk about

themes
of jumping jacks,
of battles between good and evil. Talk about
life-threatening adventures,
nine-headed hydras, three-headed dogs,
heroes reborn from the ashes who fought
the lot that talks about a setting: place and time
of little boys' delight—no princesses!
Not on lovers' quarrel

or your friends will laugh
(or whether your parents should be worried)
about the setting: place and time. Talk about

animals that talk
with clever tongues. Talk about
a sleepy rabbit under a tree,
a thirsty crow with pebbles,
a mouse with a lion's heart
that manages to speak through your heart.
A message left unspoken
and asks for interpretation
about a setting: place and time. If not, talk about

an armoured course
of CS:GO PUBG guides
of guns and loot and guns and loot and guns
that fire unlimited bullets
stacking numbers for headshot montages
action-packed with god-tier weapons
seasonal collectables, customised full-amoured glory
enough to honour the assassin's creed. Talk about
bullets made with rubber and bean-bags
in a bloody setting: place and time. But why not talk about

Hong Kong,
of everyday life,
of what you see and hear. Talk about
an experience well-felt
fresh memories of last week
or yesterday or the day before
about a setting: place and time. Talk about

walking with your family on the streets

sweet treats you bought at the park

some funny scene showed up

captured in moments on the screen. So talk about

something real

when you

talk about a city

about a setting: place and time.

2. TALK ABOUT HALLOWEEN

I was teaching them grammar
—the singulars and plurals—
when one student asked me,
what did I do for Halloween?

I wore a mask, I said, a golden one
with lines reached down like a hand.
I was dressed in black from head to toe,
a cloak around my neck, a ghost in disguise.

"But isn't it a children's thing to celebrate Halloween?"
I said, no, on the contrary,
grown-ups love to play dress-up.
I was walking on Chater Street
when I saw the carnival:
they have all sorts of clothes
from halter dresses, faux-leather skirts to skin-tight jumpsuits
150+ words in the fashion vocabulary
but not including the costumes they wear so close to their skin.

I saw Winnie the Pooh with thinning hair
holding a honey jar in his hand.
Surrounding him, a boy band in bouncer suit
escorting him across Abbey Road.
A recorder was playing in one of their pockets,
as they sang along to the Russian National Anthem.

Across the street, the Egyptian pharaohs

rose from their graves:

King Tut, Ramses and Cleopatra

gold crowns on their skull.

Standing next in line, there were the quiet nuns

that you don't see in churches;

their faces white

eyes popped out like marbles

with wrinkles so deep,

you could barely see their cheeks!

They wore a cross necklace,

a habit for cover,

and they grinned at you—never mind—

they are exactly the nuns you see in churches.

But more this year, jokers pranced around

in pantone colours—always smiling

at those who dressed up in onesies;

how often would you see

an alien walking around with a baby on its tummy?

"How weird," she said, and they walk like crabs.

But that's not all, the parade had just begun.

More people dressed in black wearing different cut-paper faces—

eyeless characters printed off from familiar TV screens.

Men in white collars who bark like dogs

who talk in high places and hold up the sky.

Sitting on the pedestal, a fox with curls

looked at the smog and called it 'blue.'

Behind the wave of Guy Fawkes masks,
face masks and more and more dog masks
followed the thousand men waiting in full-amoured gear.
A black baton dangled between their legs.
They hit you on the head
and threw cans of smoke that make you cry…
"But Daddy said it's bad to smoke."
I know, my dear, I know.
But Winnie the Pooh trapped the smoke in the jar,
the pharaohs wrote signs that put the messages across.
The nuns sent people running off the other way
while jokers and alien babysitters kept the dogs entertained…

"So what did you wear for Halloween?" I asked.
She smiled and said to me,
"I dressed up as an angel with butterfly wings."
Her name is Mia and she is seven years old.

HONG KONG WAY: A CITY WATCHING IN RELATIVE DISTANCE

14.6 kilometres is the road distance from Chai Wan to Kennedy Town,
an additional 2 kilometres if we start further at Siu Sai Wan.
To form a human chain, the safe distance between people is at least six
    feet apart,
which makes only an approximate nine thousand one hundred and
    twenty people—
one tenth of a percent of the total population of Hong Kong—to join
    hands
along pavements, waterfronts, overpasses, zebra crossings, local parks,
and light up the whole coast of Hong Kong Island with waving iPhones
    and Samsungs
from the eastern mouth of Victoria Harbour to the tenebrous waters
    of Belcher Bay.
Mooring on the other side of Tamar flickers the same stripe of light in
    Kowloon:
the reinvented Kai Tak of jutted cruise terminals, Whampoa Garden,
the Hung Hom Promenade, the Avenue of Stars and the point of Star
    Ferry Pier—
7 kilometres to a hundred years of reclaimed land (how many tons of
    gravel and sand?
the insouciant socialites have already lost count); venturing north,
the human chain continues on the grand avenue of Nathan Road
where bus stop signs and harlequin posters are more abundant than trees,
3.6 kilometres long, all the way up to Sham Shui Po and more—
8 kilometres west to Tsuen Wan Plaza, 17 kilometres east to Kowloon
    Tong, Choi Hung, Lam Tin, Yau Tong and neighbouring Tsueng
    Kwan O;
the remote New Territories shimmer from beyond the Gold Coast,

5.3 kilometres from Tin Shui Wai to Chung Fu and Siu Hong to Tuen
    Mun.
The city conduces an indomitable illumination of a total of thirty miles,
50 kilometres of collars blue and white, 2+1 nuclear families, single parents,
    grandparents, elderly in elderly homes, children in uniforms, boys
    and girls, men and women—all join together with hands united,
beaming a communal light brighter than skyscraper lights, distant stars
    and moon combined,
a total of two hundred and ten thousand people to light up Hong Kong.
Two hundred and ten thousand people.
Two hundred and ten thousand people in a city of seven million.
It only takes two hundred and ten thousand people, three percent, in a
    city of seven million,
and a city of seven million is enough to link up Hong Kong thirty-three
    times;
its distance, thirty-three times longer than the distance covered;
its light, thirty-three times brighter than two hundred and ten thousand
    mobile phones
shining on a narrow streak of land, its arbitrary borders of autonomy;
its average living space, a hundred and seventy square feet,
barely enough to sustain a living when concrete bricks are more valuable
    than gold bullion and more precious than social connection.

I look to the eponymous guardians who have outlived their time.
Their immortal shells in the name of Urban Renewal remain a spectre
    to me
where a thousand phones, torches and laser pointers could not illuminate
    a life that I did not live fifty years ago:
What does it mean to live in the squatters? To situate? To relocate?
To live in a family of many sisters and brothers, wearing the same rags
    of shirts and shorts?
To recall a reality from a TV series that I did not grow up watching?

To recall peeping through the neighbour's door and chasing comedy
    sitcoms through a gap?

To recall not owning anything, not even a box television?

To recall owning everything that does not require the expense of money?

To recall the whizzing white noise and the humming your mother
    makes in the kitchen?

To recall the soporific melody of a theme song to resonate with? To
    sing along with?

To recall the Conic radio recorder that sounds more ancient than melancholic?

To look at a yellow family photo and hold my heart to feel overwhelmingly
    nostalgic?

To find carrying a typewriter case more sentimental than typing on a
    typewriter?

To instinctively meet at the five flagpoles when you ask for a meet in
    Tsim Sha Tsui?

To prefer lying on a hard bamboo mat than sinking in a soft feather
    mattress?

To remember lying on a hard bamboo mat with your brothers and sisters?

To remember sleeping sometimes on the floor with your brothers and
    sisters?

To remember the long heat of summer and not turning on an electric
    fan?

To remember turning on an electric fan is a luxury and also costs money?

To remember the names of your neighbours and greet them whenever
    you meet?

To exchange gifts with your neighbours and celebrate on festive dates?

To offer help and take care of your neighbours' children in times of
    emergencies?

To drop off your children in times of emergencies and trust that your
    neighbours will take good care of them?

To remember breathing fresh air and living far away from the city centre?

To remember living near the hills and getting mosquito bites is a daily
    routine?

To remember seeing cockroaches and sewer rats is also a daily routine?

To remember leaving them alone is another daily routine?

To remember the restaurants remembering your name and chatty uncles talking about horses?

To remember finding a cockroach leg in your food is not a big deal?

To remember finding an extra piece of Char Siu in your food is a very big deal?

To remember saying "good morning" in the elevator and put up a smile?

To remember receiving "good morning" in the elevator and a smile to start your day?

To remember feeling sad when you did not receive "good morning" in the elevator and it was hard to put up a smile for the whole morning?

To break into tears when the once friendly streets are now filled with hatred and toxic gases?

To encourage negotiations and compromises? To compliment perseverance?

To lend out forgiveness? To receive forgiveness? To share forgiveness and be kind to one another? To listen? To be listened? To be treated as adults? To be treated with respect?

To live happy knowing that our resources are scarce?

To live in constant worry knowing that our resources are scarce and risk eviction?

To live happy knowing that even if our resources are scarce and risk eviction, we still have each other to depend on? To live happy knowing that we live a happy life?

To live a simple life knowing that life is fair? To live a simple life knowing that life is just? To live a simple life knowing that by the enterprise of hard work and labour, we are rewarded accordingly with a good salary?

To live a simple life knowing that we are making an honest living for ourselves?

To live a simple life knowing how to live a simple life?

To live a simple life knowing that we are not alone?

Standing below the Lion Rock and its spirit of redefined modern existence,
I hold on to the ones that I feel most nostalgic for and do not entirely
    comprehend:
the warmth of another's hand that I do not know,
the synchronised lights and the light that is emitting from my phone,
the synchronised sway that moves my arms, my legs and my heart
that when the song is sung and a more familiar melody resonates in
    my ear,
I will not forget this moment of temporary human connection:
of like-minded people, old and young,
standing on one immaculate piece of new symbolised rock, fifty kilometres
    and six feet apart.

WEED

Weed grows
faster than smoking them.

Flowers grinding teeth
unmasked fury facing East;
an insinuating crunch.

HANG TAN SECONDARY SCHOOL (2020-)

After Jennifer Wong's Diocesan Girls School, 1990-1997

We chant the taped refrain from little red books
and wonder if those words were our own:
Arise! The call of blood longer than the river Nile…

We heard *Ten Years* and *Chicken Rib*,
and how can we forget
the empathy box in *Blade Runner 2049*?

In Chinese history lessons, we glorify leaders
of power from Qin to Mao
when rewriting history taught us how to obey and lie.

'Global history': the black and white,
a news headline on seven-thirty excuses the right
to blindfold a child with a missing eye.

In poetry, we fall away from June,
its August sleepwalkers and umbrella stands.
We want to reconnect the Kalvitis dots.

Some of us choke in our own lungs—
it's natural, we live it.
Occasionally, we all love to bet on Mahjong.

We dream of going away
to Minecraft and Disneyland,
but by leaving, we risk the chance of never coming back.

RETURNING TO NORMALITY

Remember this day: the 18th April,
when we return our bodies to the offices
and witness the homecoming of our normality.
The turning of the wheel, the expulsion of gases,
the busy roads, passageways and bus stops
repopulated with winding queues inching forward:
Everyone is late for their first day of work.
Returning is not easy—the skin to skin action
brushing past sweaty arms and shoulders
in the intensity of the sun;
it's not the physical touch that we've been missing.
What had been a few months transpired to long-drawn mental years,
some neo-virtual inception or prolonged illusionment
lasted far too long—too long that we have sped up
the ageing process, but at what cost?
The time spent staring at the screen,
we were too late to realise
that we're no longer young anymore.
We've aged and we've grown out of sitcom comedies.

So let it be known! For it is in that liberating time
for the sorry imprisoned souls and the socially inept
to reconvene and readdress themselves to the public,
to redeem their oral fluency
and make good use of their knowledge
they have accumulated—everything is set,
waiting for this perfectly visible moment: You,
after binge-watching the epics on Netflix,
the satirical newsreel entertainment

and six episodes of Moon Knight—
You know it is worth it.
You know you splurged on between-meal snacks
and door-to-door deliveries.
You know you never worked: the twelve hours
of company service you slaved through,
the mountain of documents and off-hours meeting calls,
you are grossly overworked
and you have much to rant about.
You watch your breathing styles,
checking in for insufferable coughs and relapsing fevers
because you know you are getting infected either way
from the demons of this world
that only come out at night, the 6 pm curfews—
and we don't talk outside anymore, not for a long time…
For the sake of romance, we only speak in brief
with our thumbs dancing on the greasy keyboard.

But now we are here, allowed to meet for real,
in person, with real profiles, in medias res,
in public announcement, if only temporarily,
we get to live again. In the dimmed light
of the Social Room where it feels most comfortable
and the presence of wine (two for one till 9 pm)
we are in our nature of what things used to be:
To enter a meeting without sending a notification,
you do not have to worry about pressing 'Accept' or 'Decline'—
the mental breakdown, as you are put to wait
in a waiting room, but really only three steps away
with an almost empty glass of wine.
You are intoxicated, just about ready to enter
and engage in any social demand for talk

with a half-conscious mind
but you stand there like a plant and mute yourself completely.
With the right time, you leave a comment along the way:
a smiley face, a dubious wink,
"An eggplant for your troubles," you say,
and an occasional thumbs-up to show that you are there.

Then you are really ready: you raise your hand
for your turn to speak. You make a clink
with your empty glass because you seek attention.
You want a word, a phrase, a one-liner
that would make your presence
and let them know what you are made of!
You want to let them know you are here,
participating, with a head count for turn-taking
to avoid overlapping voices—let the man speak!
The one-liner must be significant, striking,
and command the voice of God.
You rehearse it in your mind, typed it out
on the inner linings of your brain.
You are ready to send it out by word of mouth
and announce in your loudest voice: "HEY!"

You panick. You forget what you wanted to say.
"Can I go to the toilet?" you say instead and leave the meeting.
You pull the plug and dash to a safe spot in the cubicle.
Your sanctuary. You feel your asthma working up.
So you pull out your phone again
and check for likes on Facebook and Instagram,
and suddenly, everything is all right again.
Because conversation is hard,
talking to people is hard—real people,

and your tongue doesn't work like your fingers do.
Because returning to normality is not easy,
and you realise it will take time,
and will take a lot longer—
It's going to take a lot longer
before you return back to normal.

II

Moloch!
Solitude! Filth! Ugliness!
Ashcans and unobtainable dollars!
f
o
l
l
o
w
y
our
inner
moon-
light;
don't
hide
the madness.

A SHOPPING PRAYER FOR LITTLE POSSESSIONS

You've held me to account many times in your career

to inquire the many possessions that I have to afford

a dress. "A dress!" you said. "A Bardot dress then of fine interlace!

If not the most suitable gift for your beloved wife,

girlfriend, secret lover, crush, mistress, friends with benefits—"

I left before you said another and stumbled into a second shop for you

to inquire again the many possessions that I have to afford

shoes. Necklaces. Earrings. Sunglasses. Handbags. A fucking sense of
    humour

when you pulled Van Gogh's self-portrait on a china mug, a teabag,

a three-tier stand or even a chair to sit on, 'cause why the fuck not?

None of which I have in mind enticed me to buy.

You scorned, turned away and came back yet again with a tenacious
    smile, a curtsy;

a hermaphrodite disguise of a lady in labelled dress

or a gentleman in slim cut suit, flashing a grandiose gesture

to welcome my reacclaimed noble presence, an invitatory stroll around
    your vineyards

of vintage chattels and haute couture, so you may persist

to encapsulate and wheedle my every desire,

as I wander around, in exile, a Pacific Place that you called Paradise.

Oh New Gods of Phthisis! Boucheron, Bvlgati, Prada, Chanel,

Dior, Diane Von Furstenberg—forgive me for my transgressions,

as I drag through your corridors of white, wrapped in indigenous wear:

my tattered shoes, my unbranded shirt, my second-hand trousers and
    digital Casio watch—

I am shameless! I am penniless! I am thrifty beyond belief!

Your angelical guise and suggestive stares remind me that I am tan,
your modelled bodies of diamond cuts compare to mine uncarved like
     stone,
no chiseled six-packs, no marker-drawn jawline, syringe extracted fat
     for buttocks,
I am no posing mannequin of transcendent expectations,
nor perfected with a shapely face of aspired resemblance to a snake:
you've assembled the pretty men and women in your image,
painted the ceiling to replace the sky, plotting fireflies with push-pin
     lights;
your veins surge of electricity, illuminate brighter than the sun, twenty-
     four seven,
praise thee to Edison! That when the burning ball of gas must fade
one hundred forty nine million kilometres away,
we shall have light in our cubicles and heaters in our living room!
The stores will live on to be consumed! Consumed! Consumed! As
     bamboo trees
are replanted as fences to separate tables and modern art exhausted by
     phones taking pictures.

You welcomed me with open doors, and yet, I am so displaced.
Although I cannot concede the courtesy of your lavish inquisitions,
I thank your windows of immunity, your lights in purblind darkness
when the sky was brewing a ruthless storm, the blitzkrieg struck before
     the megaphones,
the pollen burst of chemical clouds descended a downpour of pepper
     rain
that burned my eyes, my lungs, my skin, my exposed arms and legs,
you provided refuge for children like me: threadbare, bruised with swollen
     eyes,
scarred by the altercations of Reality that dominate the city
where the world beyond these heavenly doors, you've stood in equal
     standing:

Accumulate! Consume! Accumulate! Consume!
We all submit to your dollar that we cannot live without!
As you freed me in your bosom of air-conditioned halls,
quenched my thirst with your flaunting breasts of see-through windows,
you've rewired our brains to a new testament of your material values
that when we stare in the face of dehumanised mannequins,
we are obliviously looking at the coy reflections of ourselves;
for you choose for us what to wear, what to believe, what not to resist:
the desire to spend that is paradoxical to what commands our callus hands.

So I pray to ask a most humble request: to lease a kindness
and spare me free passage to walk through your corridors of white,
your Shopping Paradise that whatever you hold me to account,
I will do in return, forever in debt, pay in monthly credit card instalments.
For what I am searching for to purchase in your walls of expectation:
fifty years of promised time signed at birth that will last twenty seven
    years more.
By the the vicissitudes of life that are strapped on our backs
and the red threads of fate of Thatcherian interlace,
in the name of Fendi, Chloé and Emporio Armani,
I will surrender what I have in my little possessions:
a uni-ball Signo pen, a Gambol notebook, a tenor voice
to afford, in exchange, a Sweetworld chocolate-coated almond we called
    Freedom.

SQUARES

I

Disjunctured alleys burgeoning still a brigade of barking dogs
scavenging through the tremulous night where lowly drifters

also claim to be theirs. To which he owns a severed body
an arm of nylon RWBs that he could carry, moving

on his back a big body sack of cardboard property
of accumulated wealth which unwraps like a present, revealing

preponderant stacks of polystyrene boxes, cut-out furniture,
and set up borders of isolation for reclusive space: Do not enter. Do not

look. He chews on the discarded end of a banana peel
of which he has mistaken to be his tongue is actually his tongue

and what could be leftover bread. He turns, facing the sheltered wall,
and pulls over his head a torn habit patched and sewn with fragmented
    squares,

a child's foam mattress to lie on, contemplating repeating patterns
of triangles and circles in short episodic dreams

of tomorrow: another day of moving, of territorial stray dogs,
of blunt incisors, of lowered heads clasped between bruised kneecaps

after long begging hours and shortness of breath;
he is on his own, clinging onto that last artless will

of human kindness. He turns over the iron bowl,
deciding whether to take that extra coin. Still chewing.

II

In winter. It has
always
been the strength
of his armpits,
a raffia string
to tie up
the cardboard layers of skin
that he had lost   over the years
folded and fitted
in neatly
in a
separate
plastic bag he
labelled, among
many other things,
more
precious   in life: it is his
mattress, table and chair.
From this retangular corner   to that
is his living room. He

puts on
his moth-eaten sweaters
the smaller ones
belonged to children, who
grew out of their   renewable bodies
now piled on top of him
like a shaved knoll

covering

his exposed ribs looking fine

      living still

with

detachable   stomach

kept in another

separate

plastic bag;

the warmth of sheep wool

and cotton

for gastric satisfaction

the gift of old age

He wakes up at 4 am.

His mind unhinged

startled

by an unrestrained tranquility

in his ear, asking:

where should I find my breakfast?

III

Observe.
The modern caveman
in his natural estate. His
barefoot belongings
scream of vanity
without ownership: scratching

velcro skin that keeps on
growing barbed splinters,   hoarding
acne pillowcases to brush against
and stuffed abandoned dolls
that were losing a button, an eye or a limb
to raise his head for better sleep.

          In which he buries himself
with woolly sandpaper sweaters,
a honeycombed down coat
to shelter atop,
drenched in rainwater,
where brumous winds
leech the life out of his plastic wrappers
          to the bone—

He has no repository for celestial bonds.
Only the moon he prays to
gives him reason to speak—what of
his condition more abstruse than loneliness?
To tell which day is night

and night is day, and when he will stop
roaming and bind his feet
before Guanyin Bodhisattva.
Then be consumed in his bed
by a mountainous pile of kraft paper bags
he couldn't read: *when*
was the last time he took a shower?

He follows the way of the Nomads,
rolling past populous streets
of Argyle and East Point,
a tumbleweed as wild as we see
in Western movies. But did you also know
that they are diaspore plants?

Observe.

IV

Jeremiah sleeps legs first in a coil.
Jeremiah's toes adjoin to linger in the residual heat
of what's left functional in his failing metabolic life;
his heart barely sustained with minimal movement. Be still, Jeremiah.
Until the dawning light withdraws from the entrance
of the underground tunnel, be still and reserve
the last spoonful of yesterday's rice in your stomach to digest.
A night of street-hopping, scavenging orange bins
for grease-stained boxes; unopened
expired packagings are his loyal friends.

Jeremiah joins the precipice tiles, away from
the audacious squadrons who occupy vacant footbridges,
which can be internally too loud. Jeremiah hates
the mirror windows, avoids the neon billboard ads,
ignores the mannequins posing for someone else, not Jeremiah.
Jeremiah likes to think of nothing but himself alone.
Jeremiah sees what he thinks and fancies
the yellow M from across the road, sneaking in
the back door to sit for leftover fries.
Jeremiah likes to douse his fingers with ketchup
and suck the glorious teat of the red packet;
he would stay there all day, if only he didn't smell.
Jeremiah doesn't like the stare. Especially from children.
Jeremiah is human, after all. He tries not to lurch
when he passes through the door
and into the cold anonymity of the night
to find a new spot to settle, in case he gets comfortable.

Jeremiah wouldn't know where to go,
but he would know when he looks under a bridge
or a quiet tunnel that is dimly lit, something
someone else that has left behind—as he did—
a temporal tenancy
of noticeable clean tiles
and thoughtful reminder
that he, too, cares for sanitation
even if he forgets the *where* and *who*
and eventually thinks no more
of the *why* and *therefore*—
He lives,
and his name is Jeremiah.

POOP

There I was   stunned
as I watched   the audacity of the unholy poop
slumped   onto the ground. A soft thud
splattered   like a fried pickle on the Strip
accumulating new-found attention   in the MTR station
reverent children   in faithful uniform
pointed at
so warm   the greasy slick of damned remains

            untouchable

                   foul.

                                           crouching above
the iridescent sign   of the full moon
shone   with all its glory
a peculiar shape   of a beaver
exposed under the spotlight   wiping cheeks. Laughing gas
escaped ventilated air   CCTV cameras
looking away   to find a bug to fix
the unspeakable horror   of invisible smoke
irritates the eye   I was alone, as
the indomitable scent   of wild flames
burnt my bloody nostrils   to fucking shits and giggles
I climbed   once again
into the degenerative history   of wild monkeys and cold bathroom tiles

HONEST NEWS

You've heard the news on television.
Though be honest, really, who watches TV nowadays?
But you've heard the broadcasts,
the loud lectures on public transport,
horns, wheels, tunneling feet, screening, scrolling
up for free news! Vocal news, an accompaniment
to the convenience and economy of buses
and the mass transit railway, bold and unashamed.
Subjects that no working men or women
dare to critique in case someone is keeping score.
Yet, these blatant talk of humble human lives
can be so frequently heard and yelled out without restraint,
for the next fifteen minutes, you hear them:
these brave, astounding souls you thought are so impossible
have, in turn, become so significantly insignificant
even if no one truly takes them seriously.
It is the blabber of freedom, the Koel of existence,
the liberating quack of borderline lunacy,
and it is galvanized and told by none other than
the most brittle of bones
and the most shameless of bodies
to talk about the daily death toll.

"The numbers are growing by the thousands, Ah yung.
The screws' loose in the lot of them. Lost their teeth.
Blind eye. Brains down the drain."

"It's a fizz-bit compared to the shit across the world, Ah Keung.
Ain't nothing but a black eye pea.'

"Government's unfit to speak the o'say-way.
Keep them coming and we'll be picking bottles next."

"Them white folk are feral, ain't caring a cow's ass
if they dump their lives like trash.
Them numbers don't mean nothin'."

Man alive, you've heard them talking,
complaining, gesticulating
menacingly to break apart
the government and the entire world.
A one-man army against ad hoc crisis management
PR, CPR, PRC, BBC, ABC, TBC—
these coded things that they never care.
Though they are pro-life
and sympathise the dead, and pray
all the time, incense and all:
'I'm sorry for those who died, really.
The poor bastards never had a chance
but thank god and the devas it's not me."

Who could blame these heartfelt crimes?
These grey beards have lived long enough
to see the world devolve
into depressing hypotheticals
and survived with mere stubbornness.
They bare arms against the evening stampede
and weasel their fingers
through the sweaty stack of bodies
to touch the railing;
to claim Chinese in practice
and come up with whatever they can

to slap filial piety across your face
so as to claim a seat
out of lifelong discipline of learning and Chinese virtues.
Cuz your grandma needs the rest, her feet!
Who says the spirit of man is supposed to be plural
when people can be ever so utilitarian?
It is every man and woman for themselves:
Who could blame them?

"I'm telling you, Wu Tai, once they stop wearing them
it's all flying spit and arrows. I'm tired of getting stabbed."

"Leung Tai, your son doesn't go to school anymore?
Ain't you worried that your kid's getting dumber?"

"It's the birds. The rats. Hamsters. The dogs and cats.
They say it all, Wong. But really, it's the water. Trust me."

"I swear they're losing it. I bet you the Japs
will rise again and come for our children. It is in their blood.
I know, Ah Mo, for it is written in the stars.
Though we won't have the time to live until then."

Who else could speak as full as them?
With all their uncensored bigotries and hypocrisies
their minds have laid spread-eagled and bare.
There is no freer creature in this world
than the unhinged hunchbacks
that have proven wilder and wiser than they look.
So prick up your ears and listen
to the daily news on broadcast,
the honest news of state-wide coverage,
still alive on transmission, 24-7,
living life better than television.

SELLING FLAGS

The boy sells flags
by the MTR station; towering parent
standing behind
authoritative talk,
"Buy this flag!"
Not the boy, not a word.

I bought the flag,
dazed by the many patterns
of pasteurised schmaltz
dyed in psychedelic colours.

LIKE THAT

What did you mean, I wonder,
when you said to me:
'I didn't expect you to sound like that'?
Like that. Like all the things we've done
to gain attention, for mutual respect, to that.
Where in our previous email exchanges, back-to-back
for months (granted that you've never heard me speak)
you've seen my signature, you've seen my writing
the way I use English as my tongue and voice,
the same exact way you use yours
to speak with me.

What did you expect to see?
The foreign chineseness,
the Asian face with squinting eyes,
thus sounding like how I should in person:
a yellow boy with an exotic lisp.
You must think me dull
if I didn't show up in a Chinese tunic suit,
embroidered on in threads of gold,
the conventional inheritance in Western fashion:
for there will always be a dragon—
a fierce golden dragon—
a phoenix or Bruce Lee
crouching in a southpaw stance,
breathing from his nose an air of undefeated arrogance.
You might even think that I have a tattoo
that runs down my spine:
"When life gives you lemons drink lemonade"
a fitting proverbial drink—
the way you think it's cool like that.

But then you saw me in my clean shirt,
leather jacket and Oxford shoes:
the yellow boy with fake hipster look.
You nodded, acknowledging the 文青 in me,
made me feel like a rebel in my own culture.
You greeted me with open arms,
bow ninety degrees and breathed
a soft fatherly thrum against my face,
seven decades of good ol' western hospitality,
a British Council accent slowed down just for me.
What is your name? You said. *Yooour. Naaaame.*
I waited for the Greensleeves
I waited for you to e-nun-ci-ate.

Then when I spoke, I introduced myself in full,
the foreign tongue I mastered to reclaim
my right to be unequivocally heard;
to find in myself an unforgiving flow
of words so verbosely and variously rephrased
to attest my equal mind and character,
for what should sound and look like my unfortunate face;
to spurt out so meticulously the magnitude of details,
of superfluous flummeries and half-ass pleasantries
to show my utmost appreciation
for the inclusion of—and if not—
the only Hong Kong fiction writer
featured in your Hong Kong anthology:
I am GLAD to be here.

As I sat through the lack of Asian representations in the room,
I ponder the many possessions that begin in the mind.
Be like water, Bruce,
as we make our way through the cracks.
But then again, even I fall into these stereotypes.

HEART OF STONE

He tells you to keep a heart of stone
and tuck your sleeves as you do your shirt,
but not too tightly so
as to give people the 'wrong' idea.
He asks you not to wear purple
and put on a gentleman's suit
with a tank-top back.
"And that," he says,
"you may lift extra weights."
He trusts you to speak scarcely about it
and you are smart enough not to tell your friends.
He mentions a certain Mrs. who is too prying,
and teaches you how to dismiss her;
he teaches you how to lie.

He reminds you to stay away from the spotlight,
that it demands too much and it will burn your skin.
He implores you to refrain from attention
or the urge to look into a boy's eyes,
and yet, he'd rather see you with guys
than walking around with a group of girls;
a hot girlfriend would be an exception
and should be the *only* exception.
You should not helm the masses
when the tides are too strong;
for it is not as brave as going solo
when you are just different—
because *being* different is not easy
and fitting in is not exactly a choice.

He begs you to put aside your pride—
to give in, but not so much as to give up,
and you know what he means.
He tells you that he loves you
like a son he never had.
He begs you to stay home
He prays that you will be honest with who you are,
and goes about devoting to every religion:
he attends Sunday school and burns incense sticks.
He blames himself—
he thinks he has wronged you,
that he must have done something
abhorrent and unforgivable.
Then he says that the world is not ready yet
and asks if you would forgive him.
You nod and watch him go,
not knowing
that even a heart of stone
could also hurt this much.

THE REPTILIAN

When the Reptilian is born,
it is born without skin. Sweet flesh,
tender limbs, the odour of sour milk,
eyes bewildered by the many eyes
reflecting upon theirs: expectant, perfect.

The Reptilian is unconscious, confused
and conditioned in the composition of words.
It observes the walking chair, the Bing cherry
and the warping tapestry spinning
and unspinning on the wall:
it does not know what to think of it,
but is instinctively attracted by it.
It learns its first word borrowed from the stars—
its given name, and their names inherited from them:
it has its father's nose and its mother's eyes.
The first time it looks into the mirror
is the moment its life is given Meaning;
It is given Purpose.

The Reptilian demands sustenance:
the adults provide and it flicks its tongue,
balancing the feud between right and wrong
like hot soup on a spoon. When its instinct emerges,
it spits out aggression like fire to ants;
it severs the seams and wields the rattle like a sword.
The Reptilian is solitary and self-absorbed.
The cold-blooded creature cares only for itself:
it yearns for attention and the primates should listen.

But like a wolf spider, it has trust issues.
It cowers and whispers behind a plate of amour—
scales pointing out to bleed and keep its distance from its own:
there will only be one Reptilian, and one is enough.
The Reptilian is intelligent. The Reptilian anticipates.
It grows in patience. It learns to adapt. It deceives.
It changes skin to protect its back from behind.

The Reptilian is ephemeral and fragile, it realises.
When its mortal body moulds with old age,
it protests, its maladies fester in its every bone, and it is no longer mobile.
It soon falls over a pit of sand in the heat of extremity;
burnt, disdained by the stone and dirt of the pavement.
It reminisces then: the *is*, the *was* and what *will* become—
but it knows very well that not a breeze would care,
as it climbs into the fridge, recoils, and perishes;
its existence erases from the bitter soils of the earth
and its corpse remains, abandoned,
desiccated, in the shape of a dry cashew.

A CUTE DEPRESSION

Scrolling through the liberal space that we call the Internet,
I sometimes fancy the oxymoronic minds of the social media maniacs
    who fish for likes in exchange for recognition and sympathy,
who declare themselves depressed and compliment their bravery
when they speak outwardly of their self-diagnosed mental conditions
    with Sparkling Hearts and #MentalHealth #Blessed,
whose Declaration of Insecurities is written in flamboyant unreadable
    cursives and sprinkled on with phosphorescent butterfly dust because
    depression doesn't suit a dismal grey, but a concoction of pink fluffy
    unicorns and rainbow-coloured Froot Loops.
You beautify depression with stickers and watermark attractions, you
    dye your hair,
you paint your lips red, you put on make-up and a sexy showy dress
to stand out exposed and vulnerable on news feed live and claim the
    headline of defence against depression in repetition of the grand
    narrative like a moth to a flame
and a deceptive moth, indeed, who pretends to be a butterfly,
hopelessly addicted to the virtual spotlight of Instagrammable selfies
and suffers from a cute depression with shameless self-promotion syndrome.

You see, I do not doubt your fundraising capabilities, your handsome
    photo collages, your actual good intentions underneath the cowl
    of your pimple concealers and liquid foundations, and perhaps, you
    have more monetary contributions than any other associations
    combined that I could ever imagine—
But depression is not glorious, nor does having suicidal intents grant
    you unlimited bragging rights and make you exclusive to popular
    attention, because

those who suffer from it day-to-day do not speak of it, and how they
    swallow their bitterness without complaint, without a tear, a snivel
    or whimper, and continue to live on their lives brooding an
    insurmountable sadness in their visceral minds without seeking any
    institutional assistance:
who, with young innocence and preliminary education, hobble through
    the narrow trap alleys alone after dark and return home to a tippling
    single mother or father slapping him across the head because they
    think he is mute and mentally impaired,
who hides herself in the toilet when the ceiling collapses and is ripped
    apart by a consistent yelling and loud raging of a tempestuous
    hurricane that send remote controls, CDs and porcelain bowls
    flying across the heated room and smashing against the walls (she
    makes sure to unlock the door if her parents decide to knock),
whose arms and legs are lashed with red rattan stick marks except the
    areas where the uniform cannot cover, and is constantly reminded
    of the consequences of talking back at home whenever they sit in
    class and would rather stand behind or outside the classroom with
    an excuse that they've forgotten to bring their textbooks,
who is interrogated by a nosy social worker when life is what it is that
    doesn't need telling and now, he has to explain why he missed soccer
    practice with his friends—the only precious moment that he feels
    happy with scars and bruises,
who frantically employs her wildest imagination to fabricate a perfectly
    loving and especially hardworking Dad to explain his mysterious
    disappearance one night in her life, in case the question comes up
    in conversations or when the teachers ask her to share her family
    to the rest of the class,
who keeps a secret mirror in her wallet to remind herself to always
    smile when others are smiling, laugh when others are laughing,
    and smile still when others are sad because it's easier to look tragic
    than to look comforting, so smile! The socially inept chameleon!
    Even though you don't know how to smile,

who spends Monday, Wednesday and Saturday nights crying in the
wet pillows and on other nights occupied with what's waiting on
the other side of the door,

who finds sleeping pills a permanent cure for insomnia and alcohol an
effective erasure of childhood memories,

who find drawing on their arms and legs oddly relaxing, and start digging
through the itchy scabs because the ugly colour goes against the
colour of their skin,

who counts the number of empty beer cans in the living room and
unopened beer cans in the fridge, and calculates the estimated time
for Father to stop and regurgitate the equivalent litres of beer and
more,

who inhales Mother's tobacco in the smoky sauna living room and
observes the cheap tricks underneath the clattering green table—
whether it's Mahjong or Poker, he knows when to go all-in and
when to give out favours, but never refuse a cigarette and a good
hand in a gambling game,

who finds psychiatric pills gone from the private drawer as Mother
jumps on the sofa couches celebrating freedom, and later recovers
the blister packs from the trash along with all her friends' postcards,
crumpled and stained with food residue,

who take it to the streets with their voices cracked after hours of screaming
out the tenement windows, "I can't take this anymore!" and find
an underground tunnel or a nearby park bench to spend the night
along Oi Shun Road bitten by mosquitoes,

who is reminded when looking at the scruffy man sleeping next to
him of the time when Father pointed at a random vagrant beggar
along the street and said, "You will end up like him, beggar-boy,"
and he wonders why he did not speak up then and let Father
lecture him publicly with an obnoxious grin,

who wanders off the neighbourhood streets at midnight, crossing roads,
highways and intersections with eyes closed because the magnificent
M can be too bright on the other side spilling liquid gold,

who finds solace seeing other teens his age wandering the same
unaccounted streets; some in groups of four or five, some in pairs,
others alone, and he follows the lonely ones who seem to know
their way, but ends up walking laps around a building lot like a
goldfish in a minimalistic glass bowl with a bed of pebbles and a
short plant made of plastic,

who ventures through new unfamiliar alleys and discovers a haven of
operating computer consoles where teens who have nowhere else
to go can rent a few hours of virtual escape into the vast cosmos of
multidimensional games and play to his heart's delight,

who stays on for six hours entering lobbies to kill or be killed, respawn,
and be killed again by enemies who themselves have it hard in life
and are most probably in the same cyber bar with him, having
the thrill of it all: the punching, stabbing, bone-breaking blows,
headshots, nutshots, eyesores with bleeding screens—the joy of abuse
without physical or psychological pain in one season package is a
lost teen's orgasmic dream,

who leaves the gaming paradise unwillingly when the sun is up, smelling
of cup noodles and luncheon sweat, and decides to skip school and
go back in again begging for another six hours because the cyber
bar opens twenty-four seven and their heavenly doors will always
welcome the woebegone adolescents who need more time and
happiness to kill,

who grows up in later years, a college dropout, unemployed, still getting
yelled at by Father and Mother who have declined in years and still
busy smoking and drinking, demanding reparations because raising
him is a burden and is an obvious mistake,

who grows up hating the society for doing him dirty, for framing reasons
that blame him for being poor, for being brought up in a broken
and abusive family that made him incompetent in an absolutely
fair competition of cultural studies and monopoly because he did
it to himself! He is to blame because he is weak! He is to blame

because he is lazy! He is to blame because he has given up on
opportunities and why can't he do it when others can, some of
which are even born from grass-roots families? He is to blame for the
fact that he is spineless! He is to blame because he is the cockroach
of society! He is to blame because he believes in all of it;
who believes that wearing a pretty dress makes her feel worthy,
who believes that wearing a handsome suit gives him some sense of
control,
who believe that fixing their faces and bodies to ideal symmetrical
slender shapes would make them feel secure and loved,
who believe that enlarging their breasts and buttocks with silicone
jellies would bring them adoration and attention,
who believe that without all these accessorised embellishments and
surgical transfigurations, they will return to their worthless selves:
unloved, invisible, unimportant,
who believe that they are worth less than a dress, less than a suit, less
than any other person who walks with a straight back and with
their head up,
who believe that they are always alone and destined to always be alone,
unable to feel the warmth of a gently-tucked blanket, the homely
clement embrace from a loving parent, the nightly communion
and turn-taking thanksgiving prayers at the long dinner table…
until you come along like a fallen angel with glittery wings,
your pedicured halos of upbeat personas, your rollicking announcements
and success stories which seem too good to be true, lead to many
who emerge from their burrows of twinging melancholy, step up
and share their bitter unrepresented lives—
you've gathered more avid believers than Instagram supporters who
see you as the glamorous butterfly that they could never be…

You see, I wish I could see the fantastical world through your pretty
   eyes:
to look beyond the borderless canvas of nomadic clouds and sky and
   dream of pastel colours for abstract art,
to picture the benevolent sun and moon and the thicket of orchid trees
   switching sides with the turn of a leaf,
to find the first glacial dew in the break of day and night condense and
   evaporate from the unmistakable greenness of tropical leaves,
to flip underneath and discover a line of silver, a splash of pink and purple,
   as you place your ear against the bark and listen to the passage of
   water through its buttress roots from the well-fed ground,
to hear the sounds of your breathing and heartbeat and the perpetual
   chirping of crickets scattered along the riverbends and secluded
   hiking trails,
to sit on a log of clever mushrooms or mossless stone and embrace the
   serenity of a shallow spring with blue jewel dragonflies dancing on
   calm crystal waters,
to find the stalwart single-filed black ants scavenging for exotic foods
   beyond their nests and the buzzing bumblebees teasing ripe flower
   pollens with their toes,
to wait until the sun disappears from the horizon and find fireflies
   flickering their bottom lights in shy berry bushes—
Where are you to imagine these naturalistic analogies? When you return
   once again to the early evening crowded streets and praise the gaudy
   neon lights even if they outshine the constellations, which you call
   evidently vibrant and homely,
to pass by the flower markets and recall the smell of soft fragrant tulips
   and bluebells blooming elsewhere in vast fields and backyards when
   there are only botanical gardens and metal-framed clothesline
   apartments here,
to pet the furry tags of friendly puppies and kittens who are sheltered
   from the cruelty of abandonment and adopted life,

to hear the gentle streams of flowing tributaries if not distracted by the
loud flush of toilet water next door or the draining sewage that
runs underground,
to dream of white and thick fur coats for winter when there is no
falling snow but still cold through the castle walls made of cardboard
for the threadbare and homeless,
to dream of paradise and sympathetic angels who grant those who look
for mercy the determination to step up for the dauntless jump into
the chasm of eternity because all is good in arms of the Lord,
to open your eyes to the necessities that make up your room, your
possessions that keep you safe and calm—but when you imagine
the sun casts its light on your skin through the bedroom window,
does it warm you? Does it burn you? Does it tire you to the bone
that you don't want to wake to see another day? To wake, to sleep,
to dream, to wake up again—
Oh how wish I could compare myself to a butterfly! To bathe in the
colourful powders of Holi and fly off to Tomorrowland with a
flutter of wings and then and only then to the empty bottles of
Amitriptyline and my last reverent sip of coffee at the bottom of
my cup…
The black koel will sing on the half-hour. Will I ever be able to write
a nature so beautiful that will convince my morose and sorry mind
to believe?

WALLS

There is something within these four brick walls
within these tightly-packed compartmentalized flats
that encapsulates the old Chinese meaning of 'Family';
where we tread with care, tiptoe on planks
that make up the floorboard, and you never know
if a baby or a troubled lady is living in the flat next door.
The walls are thin, paper-thin, the only thing
that secludes us which we call our 'personal space'—
We learn by growing up
that space is valuable, precious and expensive.
We learn that space is not always private,
and a 'room' is arbitrary—
it could well be the size of a closet.

Behind those roller shutters filled with peepholes,
the modern nuclear family struggles
in a fish bowl made of glass:
we breathe in the same water
and suffocate in the same air;
We shimmy through the scanty narrow doors
as we do in life; and with our clothes reused
covered in pinholes and fuzz balls
over and over again.
Always thrift, but you see the gradient of colours
from brand-new dye to nearly white.
The patches, the smudges, the coffee stains—
a living record of your always consuming,
scorns and playful tomfoolery; memories
of your father, your mother, your brothers and sisters;

your communion at the dinner table,
reporting how your day had gone—
then you forget the space (if there was any):
the squabbles, the quarrels and unintentional trespassing,
you know it's hard to live under the same roof,
the same room, the same flat enclosed within
these four walls that we made our own.
Because we all live for the same dream:
to get out of here—this ramshackle of a den
that cannot put itself back together.

One day, we'll leave as swallows do.
Your parents will stay as part of the furniture
and bid you farewell. Until the day
you return to this empty nest,
they will want to see you fly and let them go:
They will say there is nothing left to hold you back.
They will say there is nothing to be nostalgic about.
They will say a lot of things,
and they will also say
there is nothing to be sentimental about.
But you know
there is something
within these four brick walls
that keeps you here,
and you will know in time
when you stare
up
at the ceiling
one night
and see only stars.

III

On the horizon was the moon. She fattened.
She grew huge and rusty, she mellowed and rolled,
till the morning star contended and dews began to blow in our windows
—and still we rolled.

FROM WHERE I START

From where I start or should start I do not know.
That in this moment
twice or thrice, the tip-tapping
of water finds its course
from the toilet or the kitchen
to the back of my mind.
The clockwork ticks on faster time
a quarter past; the cuckoo bird was never fixed
and was broken beyond repair.
The alley outside grumbles low
fluorescent lights flicker
        sometimes
on the ceiling
        dandruffs
               falling
               like snowflakes
        that never existed
because snowflakes don't exist
               in buildings
and the weather is too hot anyway.

But I raise my ears to the panging doors,
the escalators riding from floor
to floor, a man would walk out,
probably the caretaker doing his job, or what else
could be lurking in the corridors this late at night?
The barred gates bolted shut,
each a silver cage of its own private right.
What mischievous thoughts then

to peer in like a child,

poking through the twisted lock

with pen and tapping table knocks that never ever stop.

I hope to find a wet leg or two,

a funky sock, an unmarked screw, a pair of shoes that are not the same
    size.

To my peculiar neighbours whose secrets curb my mind:

what mysteries do you hide on the other side of mine? Afterall,

for every man obsessively keeps in possession

a quiet humming that is not quite right.

What do we see in front of the mirror

if not a reflection that diverts our eyes

from seeing the creature that is standing closely behind?

So I listen to the sounds that whisper in the night.

Poets ponder lucid dreams

scraps and shadows desire for the picking, that perhaps

when sifting through in patience would I find

not gold, but the unspeakable madness that is here:

the narcissistic woman in the form of a cat

or the clever clown that sometimes speaks what wisdom lacks.

CAFÉ NOSTALGIA

A nostalgia defines a moment of thought
when sipping a cup of Masala tea;
a moment of thought when watching it swirl,
a perennial print of where my lips were
placed, tasting of cardamom and grated ginger.
A gentle croon in a cup to stir,
smelling cathartic fumes better than city air.
Butter cookies, oatmeal muffins refill halcyon days;
the ratio of milk to tea speaks
of a dream, long-after; an afternoon, feeling right.

A nostalgia subsumes an hour of waiting,
when glancing over two long benches at the storefront,
still soaked after a heavy night's rain.
A girl had been sitting there, looking for a time.
An hour of waiting, she clasped her hands,
counting petals on the ground; she did not enter.
There were no clocks in the café, and she left
when the rain came back again.
She left her umbrella here, as well;
I took it. She didn't need it any way.

The kind store lady brought in rattan reeds
smelling of a whole bergamot tree distilled in a bottle.
A moment of thought. Another hour of waiting.
A nostalgia remits my every turn,
my every day of seeing, hearing and wondering why:
I find myself waking to read the most unsettling feed—
how many more? Nature, where poetry flows

and falls into tireless clichés—
we don't need flowers around these parts;
fantasies, too indulgent, often die too quickly.

I remember that evening I looked to the sea,
I found a dead cuttlefish on the beach.
A parent kicked sand over its body,
a three-year-old boy poked the ink sack with a branch,
stabbing it, and leaving it there.
There were no lifeguards on the beach,
just me and the cuttlefish; half-buried, still inking.
Inside the café, with good-smelling tea,
and a plague of sand flies crying louder than waves,
a vagabond still has a place to go.

RECOGNISED

You recognised me, Bobby, from across Hysan Avenue while you were
    sitting al fresco underneath a red patio umbrella sipping, I presume,
    a cup of coffee, when you texted me on the phone.
A message refreshed, a synthetic bird call resurrected the chat room
    that notified us that we have not spoken in five years;
a thinking face emoji suggested that you were wondering if it was me,
a grinning squinting face emoji suggested that you were happy to have
    spotted me regardless.
How have you been, Bobby? What have you been up to all these years?
Is your family well? Is your job going well? I presume it is, when you
    had the time to enjoy a cup of coffee on a Thursday afternoon or
    it might have just been your day-off, but who has a day-off on
    Thursday? I wouldn't know.
The last conversation we had, we ended with "hope to see you soon."
    and "keep in touch." The rest was stripped out of context like when
    you asked me, "chicken or duck?" I answered, "Jubilee, Felicity and
    Serendipity," followed by "Psychotherapy in Social Science, and
    you?" You didn't reply and called Kevin crazy two weeks later.
    (Who is Kevin anyway?)
We were probably classmates in secondary school. We might even be
    best friends once, if not, acquaintances in life, or else why would
    you have texted me, recognised me, and why didn't you come and
    say hi to me in person?

How did you recognise me, Bobby? How did you know that it was me?
    How did you know that it was nobody else, but me?
Did you recognise the blue cashew pattern design on the inside collar
    band of my shirt? How I wore it with my sleeves rolled up, untucked,
    and a pair of black slim-cut trousers and brown faux leather shoes?

Did you see me in my casual clothes, wearing a random, non-random
  oversized white Supreme T-shirt with beach pants, flip-flops and a
  golden watch that shows more than just the time?
Did you see me wearing a bandana, a red apron around my neck, holding
  a cardboard box or crate of god-knows-what that would most likely
  be groceries?
Did you see me wearing a bucket hat, a pair of cool sunglasses and a
  thick wool Korean sweater that seems to be impervious to sweat
  and resists the thirty degrees summer heat in Hong Kong?
Did you see me in a rush? Was I slipping through the inescapable crowd
  of pedestrians accumulating on the streets? Was I sprinting precariously
  on speedy roads alongside taxis in flight and rumbling delivery trucks
  running errands?
Or was I walking slowly with eyes flitting from one animated inanimate
  object to another, watching dancing teens jumping in flashy billboards
  that make up the city building walls? Was I playing an immortal
  game of spotting the difference between modelling teens and modelling
  mannequins? Was I so transfixed in my own imagination that I
  bumped into a grumpy businessperson who scorned at me, an elderly
  with a walking stick who stabbed my toes, a mindless child (like
  me) refusing to watch the road, a pissing dog who was peacefully
  watering a nearby fire hydrant or an innocent light pole that didn't
  do anything until I slammed my face and left with a dusty mark?
Did you see me skipping with music wherever I go? Did you hear me
  humming to the voltaic melody in my earphones? Did you hear the
  progression of musical arrangements and harmony in city noise?
Was I composing a smile? Was I mulling a frown? Was I laughing
  hysterically all by myself? Was I in a mood for rain? Was I stumbling
  and limping on one shorter leg? Was I nervously embarrassed by
  my awkward social interactions?
Oh Bobby, I could have been passing through with or without purpose,
  wandering the streets with a pendulum sway; a tote bag hanging

between my legs, on my shoulders, in my hand that read, "Ogier,"
with a seedling sprouting from a green earth that looks prettier
than in real life.
Or did you happen to recognise my face? Half of my face? A third?
Perhaps a quarter where you see my lock of hair falling from the
side to my nose; something straight, something curly, something
wavy, something frizzy, maybe, if I was half-awake, the stubborn
cowlick would suspend and spiral in all directions, invincible against
a full-power blow dryer and the auxiliary press of a vent brush.
Did you capture the contours of my face? My incredulous jawbone?
My cheeks that make me look puffy and skinny depending on camera
angles? My ordinary chin that does not cleft but doubles if I look
down upon my unsurprising chest?
Did you recognise my monolid eyes when I blink? My eyebrows that
look like they were drawn with shapely lines from afar, but they
are, in fact, bushy and untrimmed if they are magnified?
Or did you recognise only a glimpse? A brief image of me really running
across the street, and all the contours and features of my face and
body merged together in an instant grey; a phantom without form,
flashing from the corner of your eye in the unequivocal light of
day—what coincidence! What wonderful surprise! What mind-
boggling chance for you to remember me and recognise me from
a distance among all the people you know!

But did you know, Bobby, that I have lost my bearings in life? That the
fantastical pursuit of dreams is not as pleasant and promising as the
symbolic path that we envisioned in our younger years, and that
there was no visible route: no side barriers, no indicative blocks
that show us a direct course to proceed and follow?
That we might as well roam in the dark in an endless woodless city
and blind ourselves with overworking hours of screen time and
lack of sleep?

That I actually slaved through these laborious hours of screen time
  and lack of sleep and am slowly going blind?
Since when did I submit to the monotony and mundanity of work?
Since when did I lose my flare and dreams that had once kept me going?
Since when did my stomach forget the need of nourishment and my
  blood depend on a one-month saline drip?
Did you know that hospitals have hypnotising lights, Bobby?
Did you know that hospitals ventilate air that cleans your lungs just as
  casinos fill you up with oxygen?
Did you know that nurses talk to you, but also talk in secret code without
  you knowing?
Did you know that patients leave without saying where they are actually
  going?
Did you know that you will get used to the cold hospital air, the long
  needle stuck in the back of your hand, the empty hospital beds
  that keep on changing faces, and the frequent sampling of blood
  that you never thought you could endure and produce?
But did you know, Bobby, that I have an irremediable heart for Poetry?
The many nights that I've spent awake and writing with my muse,
  my caffeine and my dependable lamp lights, pouring my heart out
  until the holy, lustrous and immaculate yoke rises from beyond the
  quiet hills where the Old Man Rock meets the sky?
Did you know how long I've been waiting for the brilliant sun to cast
  its light upon the concrete city and bleed through the blinds to comfort
  my heavy and weary eyes?
And yet, how many people have come to depreciate the value of Poetry?
  To declare money as their only moral incentive of calculable worth
  and business as their true, preeminent religion?
Did you know how many have called me mad? Teased me, mocked
  me, belittled me for chasing an impossible dream beyond the horizon
  and the worst ones are often those who are closest to me?

Should I feel shameful of my affections? Should I be trialed for my
   ambivalence and illegal poetic constructions? Should I continue
   when I know I cannot turn away from the forceful hand of Reality
   and its predestined societal expectations? Should I be wary that on
   this lonely path, I am at the brink of losing my mind?

Oh Bobby, what do you look like now? Does your face reflect an
   older expression than what is your actual age? Do your eyes sink
   like mine? Does your head burrow inside your chest? Can you
   breathe?
Does your nose react to the new allergies from the increase exposure
   to exhaust gas and cigarette butts? Do you remember the smell of
   trees without insecticides? Do you remember the smell of rivers
   without sewage and chlorine?
Do your ears pop at the noise of traffic? Do you hear anything or
   have you gotten used to contagious car horns retorting one another?
   Do you hear the brown sparrows under your feet, scavenging for
   bread crumbs and tissue paper?
Does your coffee taste bitter as it is supposed to? Does it taste sweeter
   when you add in sugar? How much sugar do you usually add in
   your coffee to make it palatable? Does it taste like anything? Did
   you also lose your sense of taste?
Are you wearing a suit and tie? A T-shirt? A bucket hat? A pair of leather
   shoes? Flip-flops?
Is your hair slanted on one side? Slicked-back? Short and messy? Or
   do you not have hair or perhaps, already losing hair because of
   overworking, a lack of sleep and stress? Did you grow a beard?
Do you carry an impossible weight in your heart, as you sip your cup
   of tasteless coffee and contemplate on the morbid anxieties of Life?
Do you subconsciously tap your feet, shake your leg, bite your fingernails,
   check your phone because you're always insecure with missed messages?

Are you thinking, Bobby? Are thinking away from the city? Are you
    thinking of travelling to a different country with skiing and snow,
    a different city with Broadway and musicals, a different town with
    like-minded people coming from around the world in search
    for Nature, Peace and Solitude? Are you thinking of lying on a
    meadow of edible grass? A white-sand beach with see-through
    lagoons and odourless waves? Or are you just thinking in the café?
    An open, private, go-to spot along Hysan Avenue where only
    you can gain access to? Your thinking table, your thinking chair,
    your thinking arm supporting the weight of your head, thinking
    lightly…
Are you dreaming, Bobby? Does your mind wander like mine? Do
    you see the man with the beret walking backwards in the mirror?
    Do you see the woman wearing different-sized shoes and holding
    three fish scale handbags around her neck? Do you see the posing
    men and disguised women made of plastic and wood? Did you see
    a white mannequin walking out of the shopping mall, past the taxi
    stand and leave an arm raised in the air to catch your eye?
Truth is, Bobby, I was never there at Hysan Avenue.
Truth is, Bobby, I stayed home on Thursday and didn't know know where
    to go.
Truth is, Bobby, I've already forgotten who you are.
Yet you recognised me from afar among all these people—
the random, non-random person you actually saw and had mistaken
    to be me—
and still you blamed me and called me blind for not being able to
    recognise you.

PICKLED CHICKEN'S FEET

The city I live in has stranger things called food:
pickled chicken's feet,
geese, if you want an upgrade
but still also feet;
or that of a pig boiled in darker liquid,
the ginger rids the smell
when eating more skin and more lard than meat.
Juicy bacon from the lips of a duck—
tongue, to be precise—
might stop your mouth from watering…
but why not a whole cow's feast?
A stew of liver, heart and lungs,
cold ox tongue again
on the side
with sweet and sour sauce.

Around the corner, a reptilian shop serves colder blood:
snake stew, snake soup, snake heart still beating,
clinging to the side of a bowl.
They say it takes a man to stand the bitter taste.
They also say that snake tastes like chicken,
as they take a shot of the wine
poured from the jar with chopped-up spines on display.
(But I'd say it's better than the shop next door:
the black tortoise jelly often carries an odd familial aftertaste;
who could have thought that the cure for smallpox
is swimming in the fish tank of your living room?)

Then there are those that are full of hot air:
Buns freshly baked without pineapples for taste.
No piglets, no cocktails, nor a wife for that matter;
as you would expect an angry husband
chopping fine pieces
to make their beloved sweetheart cakes.
But there are cat ear crisps,
horsies and deep fried couples
that will start your day with a wonderful crunch.

Then finally there are the smaller and stranger things:
half a piece of salted egg,
a lonely stalk of veg,
a clothesline of salted fish
ready to be sucked, only rarely
but sometimes barbecue pork,
and a lot, a lot of onions
with pickled chicken's feet,
and my own personal favourite:
soy sauce with rice.

The city I live in has stranger things called food
but also sentient things
among non-sentient sort of things.

MIDNIGHT WALKING ON TAI ON STREET

Midnight walking on Tai On Street,
I happen to look up and see from across:
a bridge that hangs overhead
from one side of the street to the other.
            Stepping stones spiral up unmarked staircases
      a discontinued line of fluorescent tubes
         holds up half the ceiling,
            projecting
      a curve of one moonlit brow
         revitalised
with punk rock aerosol, Lennon Post-It Notes and stencil graffiti;
      a lambent presence
still ample to produce a phosphorus glow. Yet
                the bridge remains unnoticed
      to the weary travellers
         who bowed their heavy heads
      beneath the flickering traffic lights, unsung;
         who would rather take the straightway across
      than one that requires the extra lift upwards and down.
An awry pigeon perches on the ledge,
      moulting in soft cuckoos;
      a familiar nest humming across the road
"When Swallows Return" and is never heard.

              But like the eyebrow above the eye,
it pleases a reflection my mother longs to remember:
a warming time when she worked as a clerk, returning
         to the smell of hot soup noodles.

The holler of street hawkers with moving carts,
            tables flipped from under the bridge up all the way
                to the other side;
                    a communal space in a bowl of cart noodles
                    for all blue-collars and workers alike.
                Braised mushrooms, brisket and turnip,
                                    my mother's favourite—
        she taught me how to eat them
        with a steamy bowl she brought home every night:
            a pair of wooden chopsticks,
            a plastic spoon,
            and a stool by the dinner table I sat with my right leg up.
    "It was never the same," she said to me once,
    "Not the same feeling without the running of rats
            and cockroaches on your broken flip-flops."
    She should be asleep by now, counting away,
    and since I grew up, we've never talked like that anymore.

                            Across the flickering traffic lights and weary
                            travellers who withered and yawned,
                I go back the other way into Tai On Building
            and look for a bowl of cart noodles that doesn't taste the same.
    I will walk up the spiral steps and pass the moonlit bridge that
        cuckoos overhead,
                    and I will wait
                                    for a midnight returning
                        of chalk and Spring
                    that will come once upon a time

FIND THE FISH DWELLERS

Before there are live chickens, bundled-up vegetables,
and fresh butchers' cuts on meat hanging hooks,
there were the fish stalls. Fish dwellers reeled in seasonal catches
from barrel-loaded trucks; blue containers filled
with yellow fin breams, grey mullets, threadfins—
just to name a few: all caught
at the continental shelf of the South and East China Seas.
"Find the fish dwellers on Kam Wa Street," my grandfather said to me.
"The fish are the freshest at 4 am."
So I went to the wet market to find the fish dwellers,
where restauranteurs gathered and surveyed
the best batch of fish for the day to serve on their menus—but I was
    too late.
By midday or afternoon, the trucks were gone
and lying out on polystyrene boxes, clingy flies hovered
over classified lots, sections and space for leftover fish,
scaling intimate bodies of cold embrace upwards… Upwards!
away from ground burials, which are prone to floods of melting ice
and then of smell, sunken, cloudy, losing shine.
The fish is unpurchasable after death; and I returned home, empty-
    handed.

"Once upon a time, there were two families," my mother said.
"Five butcher daughters waited at the door
for the five-pound bag your grandfather brought home every night:
a bag full of shellfish, sometimes prawns, sometimes clams ˥—
engagement gifts from our neighbour,
five fish dweller sons to your grandfather's five butcher daughters."
A lucky match, where my mother confessed

that sometimes they peered in for the fish dweller boys
on the other side of the room: so young, robust and handsomely built.
"But your grandfather disagreed
and found only fresh seafood in a bag;
for a bag of seafood offers no less than five pounds,
but nothing more that they couldn't afford."
"'Study hard in school,' so your grandfather said.
His lifelong regret was not being able to read or write,
and he hoped for his daughters to grow up
without the sweat and hard labour
that every morning a butcher needs to carry:
the handle of a butcher's knife
and the weight of a butchered pig on his back."

My mother took these words by heart, and I learned, as well,
to find the fish dwellers for the freshest fish,
and I also understood what pleases my grandfather most:
not a tiger grouper, but whether I could wield a ballpoint pen.

ORANGE

The orange my grandfather peels off
blooms like a flower
unrolling sleeves
he presses between the whiter skin
six pieces
revealing the plump juicy bulb
that feeds our contempt and eager eyes.

The harvest of this meaty fruit
he said, depends on time.
The upbringing, if done properly—
the citrus skin when gently squeezed
breaks into the air
suspend like floating crystals, sparkling,
disappearing and sparkling again
out of nothing
too loud, too brash.

The fragrant pulps bursting out flavors
juices overflowing—sweet nectar
accumulated at its heart.
The years took to ripen the taste,
my grandfather picked them
pressed its temples
to find the perfect suitors
for his sons and daughters.

I picked up an orange and followed his hands.
Piercing through the walls with my fingernails,
the delicate skin tore apart in halves,
giving way for the careless aftermath
of brute-force incision
that sent juices spraying like a wild hurricane
across the table, the chairs and wooden floor—
I licked the messy bulb in my hand.
It burned my tongue:
too sour, too bitter.

But then he took a bite
and smiled at the first orange I opened—
the sweetest orange he had ever had.

AGAIN SOMEDAY ON BREAKING TIDES

Ye Ye, the ocean is loud by the docks tonight.
Down slippery stairs where the waters turn,
the warring tides rise above the mound
and wet my naked feet. A rush of waves
and barnacles pop at the cold breach of air,
then submerge again, the doleful gush and groans:
the ocean buries all organic sounds.
In the bay, a fleet of sampans are holding still,
and I stand where you stood
along the restless coastline, thinking of you.

Ye Ye, you would have been ninety-seven this year.
I've counted them, as you would, waiting
for the Sundays at church when our eyes finally met.
You extended an arm, your calloused fingers
caressed my cheek, and every time, I listened
to your trembling words whisper softly to me like a psalm.
Ye Ye, I knew you couldn't speak without teeth,
nor would you stand being tied down to a wheelchair,
but you were never bound by your aging body, were you:
when you stood up and embraced me with your cold, steady hands?

Ye Ye, I knew it took more than just bravery
to climb over the rails, and God knows how
I'd cried the night they trawled you out like a fish.
The ocean cleared your veins, anointed your eyes
with sand, and your skin was bleached white as snow.
They said you had fallen on your knees

and the ocean took away your pain.
They said you were touched by seaweed.
They said it was an angel that freed you from your rickety bones.
You didn't tell me that you were holding on for dear life.

Ye Ye, I wonder if your weight has ever lifted,
when you reached to the bottom and stared
up at the moonless night sky, were you at peace?
If you'd cried, I wouldn't have known,
and I was told you've never dropped a single tear.
As you drew your last breath as I did mine,
I miss you, *Ye Ye*, as I stand
at the edge of the dock tonight,
stifled by all the blistering noise,
I know we'll meet again someday on breaking tides.

MOTHER

Is it not familiar to see those messy curls?

When you first opened your eyes, she stroked your hair.

Fingers deep, caressed and gently lifted

with Ah Mah's comb in her hand.

She kneeled before the old mahogany, the raised platform

enshrined above: a lady dressed in white.

She prayed—the many years she kept her faith

and the many years of peace that was promised to her.

Her heart stayed reverent

as the orange that was placed on the table-top, just ripe.

Oh how her weakly shoulders burdened her knees…

weighing down on her brittle bones,

the worried wounds worn and torn

that by mere walking would cause her pain:

the pain in her back that she could not reach.

Moving under her feet, the scorching heat rose

from beneath the ground and appeared,

anchored between her brows.

The weave of her sweat marked the long weary path

where she used to tread along in her white rice fishes—

the "Tek Tor" flips she wore to the wet market.

Then returning home with a handful:

a pound of meat, some pak choi,

and a few salted duck eggs if not handsomely priced.

A head-hard bargain she took pride in

and a smile persevered with the will of a mother's strive.

You hurried to the front. Shoes undone.
You kicked them off, sprinted across the pavement
like the little kid you were. Battered bruises,
shirt untucked, she picked you up
and you stumbled again on the ground.
Falling, as to be grazed or ungrazed
if you had worn longer socks.

Is it not familiar to see those messy curls?
Her eyes affixed, like the loving mother
she once was—from the little boys and girls
she saw through the window
to the little footprints and fingerprints on the windowpane.
Knowing you'll grow up one day
when you look back
at those passing moments
that made her proud.
The smile in your own reflection
and the ring on your finger that is placed, just right.

NO PICKING WITH TOOTHPICKS

"No picking with toothpicks," my mother said to me.
"Of course," I replied, poking my bleeding thumb.
I stared at the hole on the wall—
fossils I found with translucent bodies
peeping through the wide opening that is the hole.
Did I say 'wide'? I meant small.
The toothpick was thin enough to do the job.

An itch. A stir. A rash on my neck
marked the time I had to stay at home.
"Stay at home," my mother said, as I
poked a hole in the wall with another toothpick—
"No toothpicks," my mother said again, and hit my hand.

What am I to do, but to stare blankly at the wall—
the wall that had a hole on it, wider now—
Did I say 'wider'? I meant smaller.
The turns of time have asked me to lie,
a transcendence to adulthood, as all adults do:
nagging, scolding, bickering father and mother
always talking, arguing, confuting issues
too big for my teeny-tiny head, but never
about the hole on the wall I picked with my toothpick.

So I took them, burnt them, threw them away
in the rubbish bin, and that was that.
"No more toothpicks," I said to my mother.
"No more toothpicks," I said to my father.
No more toothpicks for myself;

Red spots, infectious dots ripe for the picking,
like the grapes you bought from Japan,
or the bites I got when I was lying on my bed—
"No more," I said. "No more."

Then my father reached out
one Friday night
a slither of meat stuck between his molars;
a slimy slick of vegetable clung onto his two front teeth
in need of a toothpick…
Now what say you, Mother?
What say you?

BETWEEN WORDS

I was told to dream in the spaces between
words. *Run along now, son*—as I would
up a flight of stairs, tracing back to that one

unequivocal table found at the back of my exercise book
reciting mnemonic phrases of nine-times-nine, of literary
mathematical ingenuity that makes everything straight-

forward. From the point I learned to write my first
word—not on a line, but in squares—I copied ten times
connecting dots to the proportional character that is larger than

me. I've come to find the future set in due course,
as you promised, obliged your reprimand of Strays,
to warn me that *the only failure is an illiterate one,*

son. But the moment I went out of bounds was the most
liberating feeling. At some point I've grown and learned
to squabble and scribble my own staccatos for a brevity

to pause in silence. Did you know, Father,
that when I look back, I find only grey?
As plain as those uniform halls I passed through
unnoticed, too obsessed with the climb:

some chose to walk, some in a sprint—
occasionally tripping—others crawled
and climbed after one step at a time, and I

was the one who turned around, midway,

where I erased the pencil marks

to map my own and sought the colours I left behind

LESSER GRASS

Lesser each day the small patch of grass
grows thinner on my desk.
Wild weeds of course
my mother plucked them
from its roots to let the orchids grow
until the orchids died too.
The soiled pot sterilised
smelling like embalming liquids
now gained access across my bedroom floor.

Tucking in cotton sheets where sometimes
I felt like walking on moving sand
but never warm.
Standing before family pictures
I would expect some reminiscence
of the boy who smiles
who grew up lesser smiles each day.
As unfortunate sounds bicker through the doors
and walls in-between,
I forced myself beneath my skin
to sleep every night on distant floors.

The carpet I imagined whispers to me
that the lesser days I spent unperplexed
I would ultimately fit in some battered course
fists aiming for the hardest wall.
By the time I thought to myself,
"Well that's fucking enough."
I will punch some more until my knuckles ache and bleed.

"Make haste then," I said,
but not yet managed the challenges ahead.
While pioneers are fighting headstrong against the currents,
I fear the prospect of my wallet that I couldn't afford.

The dangerous state of lesser rights
low-paying jobs: a de facto testament
along Chater Road burst into flames. Standing idle,
the central bank lifts up half the sky; on the side,
a sinister blade ready to cut foreign ties.
My father's suggestive and authoritative kind
crowned the red jewel to set affix
my euphoric deranged state of mind
if need be provide a standard license
from father to son: that I, the son,
must honour my duties
to receive a well-deserved royal beating.

A voice, I had none,
as the cluster of lesser grass
grew lesser every day, plucked from its roots.
But I will help it grow until my mother
finds that same patch of lesser grass
in every pot of plant
and she would say,
"What the fuck are you doing?"

I will reply that my job is not done:
the city was ill well before it all began
when the untouched land was rare and grand
with the cluster of lesser grass
growing among the other grass and trees.

That those other grass and trees

are growing lesser each day, and lesser

when you pluck them, poison them and beat them dry

that even your orchids will die and they did—

on that very soil

that unfamiliar soil you took pride in

smeared with chemicals

but growing still

the lesser grass

on my desk

will continue

to spread

across my bedroom floor.

IV

It's that time of night,
lying in bed,
thinking
what you really think,
making the private world public.

INSOMNIACS

I

The trick
I've learned
to closing my eyes
is to keep them
open
and find
all meaningful
patterns in life
just
to be
disappointed

strained for
screening too
much
refillable water
in coffee-stained cup
tastes
just as   bland.

II

The hand of the clock
moves in one regular
beat in time,
where it posits
a calculable distance
between the last
relative second
to the next.
Just as I wonder
how words
are read
from one way
to another. Yet how is it
that when I count the time
in my heart, it runs faster
on suspension, slower
when pulling
a blank exorbitant space
over my head and find it
different, haphazard, crumbling
and deteriorating
every day

and repeat?

III

Real voices reeling in soft
sweet hums of solitude
reeling in real voices
of fish in water.
Minimalistic tank
oxygenated
with buzzing filters
to allow
perpetual breathing,
as long as the battery
and hornwort
sustain themselves.

Air bubbles release
from suction lips, rise
like miniature
marble spheres—
stored vibrations
encapsulated
to connect in chains.
Then in contact
upon its eventual approach
to touch and pop
on the cold
cold surface
where membrane
breaks in-between,
into silver shards
and stirs—

an invitation to calamity.
That in the breaking
of the early womb,
the aquatic room
sinks to writhe
and turn
to see it translate
into ghosts in my mind—
and I will, simply,
stand by the fish tank
for hours: my ears
against its inflating belly,
reeling in soft
real voices
and then some,
and then—
there was none.

IV

Waking
to a blank
stare
a crooked bird
bounced
off
from
one branch
to another
and into
my room then
when the walls
moved in
a little
closer
scurrying across
a gecko or
cockroach or
something
of
some
other *kind*
in my eye—
I blinked.

Windows locked
the crooked bird
left the scare-
crow

sheening
in the dark
and I,
betrayed
by my
unsteady
mind.

V

How a dredger berths so near the promenade still puzzles me:
its shapely hull half-floating like a beached whale,
leans stock-still against the waves and rock.
Its anchor has not emerged in days.
Its metal claw drying in the wind, still dripping
seaweed ripped off from sedimentary floor. Some
acorn barnacles click at the sound of spuming pores
rising with the tide into every bedridden chamber.
You can taste the ocean and rust;
a tang on every part of your tongue
to every part of the machinery, burgeoning
in that hollow gargantuan
of a stomach that billows and swells,
booming, as the harbour overflows with extra weight.

You wonder if it has grown on you:
as you stand by your bedside window,
watching it regress in solitude, looking far
and deep like an old man out
in the vast blue that is darkening,
and seagulls circling the mast like flies
refusing to perch or leave.

The young has heard it once.
Its stern metal frame set in due course
now lurches in abandonment. Then you hear it:
some quiet turbine turning
blended in the shallow waters

and washing of waves, the rigging
shudders beneath the silt and grime:
there is life alight the unmanned carrier,
waiting for that long anticipated horn
to reverberate in the night sky and fall down
in a ululating cloud of rain,
silent functioning—
that even something inanimate,
can be so intimidating,
daunting, and moving slowly into the night.

WHERE THE GRASS IS

greener, plateaus rise beyond the carbon-
smelling concrete higher than any skyscraper
and unmanned scaffolding.
At the foot of the mesa, the school bells
ring on the half hour, we hear
the choirs chant and praise in song
about the promise of the other land—above,
separated by a ring of clouds,
an empyrean of peace, felicity and more.

We look to the skies when we walk out
the door—any door—and our eyes
naturally roll up to find and dream
of where the grass was once sown in fertile soil,
carried along free-spirited in the wind
and not confined in pots:
where there is pollen, there is grass—and on
the plateaus, the grass is plenty,
nourished by the high mountain air
and is let to grow in disparate lengths.
Its tillers weave together into a green mat
soft and bountiful by nature's design—
the grass is sentimental,
as we were as children born to crawl on all fours
with naked hands and feet;
they do not need shoes to feel the earth.
Give them crayons and they will draw
their little imaginary worlds
with their clumsy fingers

and wobbly lines in seamless streams
and doodling flowers
that overpass
white paper boundaries
and onto the desk
with colours
in the form of renewable circles
to where the grass is greener—unlike

this: below, a group of mountaineers
struggle to climb onto every piece of rock
by their own instruments of progress built in stone
and speculation: roads doubled, tripled in size;
merchandise sold and resold by the dozen,
consumed and wasted to be accumulated
by the number of landfills and rubbish bins—
the city falls in a congestion of noises
and brown air clogged by an incessant smog
they do not know where it comes from.
A constant fear for blistering rains to appear:
they burn, as wallpaper peels off
like an overstayed Band-Aid, rivers
polluted deemed unsafe to drink—
nothing could be done:
no refillable cement
or closed-down factories could mend
the seized acres of reclaimed sea and land.

We have lost the scent of fresh grass,
as we have forgotten what grass is,
or hear the sound of birds
calling, wallowing and ardently attesting

to a garden of Eden on a plateau beyond the clouds
and we climb: our soles bruised
with the baggage we carry
and the heavy weight of the wilting world
behind our backs, asking for forgiveness.
That one day if I arrive,
I will burst into tears
at the unimaginable vastness
that I see on and beyond the brilliant horizon;
where the endless streams of Jordan
flow more than sufficient,
and a grass greener than any propane
and fluorescent aerosol spray—
radiant, redeeming, and teeming with life.

YOURS

It was my eternal morning to yours, of dreaming
in the one-hour train submerged expectantly to the thought
of your thoughts in mine, tired nights
where you rest your head on my shoulder, breathing
metronomic clouds. I imagined you toss and turn in bed, doe-eyed,
sobbing to return to your pillow yet so stubbornly awake
to drag your legs across the wooden floor
and proclaim your rights in the kitchen for a cup of freshly brewed coffee.
I imagined where your fingers stumble on the keyboard
of your faulty phone, the way you pull
your hair like clothes lines, like cotton twine, like grilled cheese,
a lock of hair half-covering your face, drooping slightly
on the side of your cheek. You never fold your blanket
and it stays exactly the way you wanted it.
What was the first thing that comes to your mind?
When you opened your eyes and saw for a glimpse
a blast of splendid colors and you closed them
to distinguish an auxiliary pattern merged in a single photograph?
Where you moved your arms and then your limbs, curled up like a child,
and your feet folded up underneath the sheets to keep them warm,
what were you holding in the cherry of your palm? Your heart,
which carries the weight of your shoulders and back? (Does it hurt?)
Do you murmur in your sleep? Does your mind spiel like a spinning
    mule?
Do you hear the oscillating winds outside your bedroom window?
Do you hear your curtains rustle with a chase of Russet sparrows?
Do you hear the wash of waves? A cave with an air pocket ready to pop?
We buried our heads in the sand, looking out for the white torches at
    the brim of the ocean,

Oh, how those slow-moving freighters slip through the docks with
  their massive bodies…
Are you awake? Do you see me leaning against the railing along the
  promenade?
But you were already standing at the lobby, weren't you?
waiting to run into my arms

ANOTHER

There she told me she loves another woman:

another woman of younger age

dreaming in her unageing twenties,

free to roam with her faithful guitar filled with decal stickers,

reminiscing the cities and streets she toured

and people she loved and fell out of love.

She wears her youth around her wrist

her arms covered with handbands, trinkets and bangles—

souvenirs from another time, another place, still definite and indelible.

She has a freedom tattoo on her left shoulder,

a winding signature on her right arm,

and something poetic between her collar bones

that she lives by and lives up to.

She would dwell in the realm of music

and marry her harmonic strings

with her nimble delicate fingers, swiping right.

Look how they dance! Look how they skip at the tip of her tongue

quiver and curve at the rolling sound of Rs

and the lyrics she wrote all by herself at night—

peaceful nights with a glass of wine, refilling

a bed full of invites to late-night shows, carouses and gigs

where she could perform uncaged, unfettered, and with free emancipation

to pour her heart out and another rue ready to be listened to;

she would be a nightingale in her past life

drifting in an endless river

and she would be beautiful, she would be divine,

she would be radiant, lively, funny and everything—that is not her.

But I see the trusted look in her eyes, the offbeat strum
that sometimes glow a reassurance
of something sanguine, something brilliant
beyond what drives this bitter sadness, which plagues her mind.
That when she sometimes wanders off to dream
and think with her fingers, drawing circles and lines
along the slight indentations on the table,
her lips do shrivel, a squeeze to remind herself
to not get distracted by the amenities in her phone.
I wonder what music does she see from her eyes,
the beginning of a note that links to another
to form a melody of sentimental tunes. Does she ever tap her teeth?
Does she ever hum when she walks? Does she live her life with
    rambunctious jazz?
As I watch her paint Abbott on her plate with a torn piece of bread
and the handbands she wears every day on her arm,
reminiscing the places that she, too, has been to, I keep in place.
Because you should have seen her smile
when she wears a Pink Floyd t-shirt with pride
and laughs with a flu shot in her arm
taking effect by the hour
and I love her
for being the silly and pretty kind.

THE PEEL STREET POETS OF OUR TIME

The pendant lights were dim in the twilight hours of Peel Street
Wednesday when we reconvened in the Social Room before the
magnanimous sight of Poetry—
a couple of early risers from work, Daniel Hamilton, Sam Powley, Trevett
Allen, including myself, were speaking passionately about the
captivations of the empowering mic and stage, and the hereditary
gift of Poetry that we are so fortunately blessed with in our time of
ephemeral existence compared to the immortality of scripture and
books lasting a thousand years;
I indulged myself with a glass of red wine and listened attentively to the
seasoned poets standing around the tall table at the corner of the
half-lit bar, going anywhere their fantastic minds and culmination
of experience took me that took them a lifetime to ruminate and
grow a magnificent beard,
when I heard someone ask a bottle of Stella Artois: where have all the
poets gone?
Where have all the poets of our generation gone? Where's Homer? Where's
Shakespeare?
Where are the Kerouacs, the Ginsbergs, the Burroughs, the spontaneous
Beats of our Time?
Where have all the modern classics gone? Newspapers that preach and
pursue the ethics of the Empirical, the Impartial, the Unimpeachable
Truth to which we depend on?
To which we read on the busy underground train to work? To instigate
social exchange with a scandalous A-1 headline? To absorb? To
evaluate? To analyse? To criticise the authority of News and Truth
itself and stir a train of pious believers who read the same news
every day and cover their fingertips with satisfied ink stains? (He
was really talking about readers and readers turn poets and he was
still very sober.)

The Future! He exclaimed and stopped at the crack of his voice with the
first alcoholic sip of enlightenment; challenging, not to ridicule, nor
to haul a peremptory proposition by the ear, but to find the visible
reactions from the bearded batch, one of grey, and I amongst them—a
young witness of the 21st century—simply shook our heads in
contemplation, saddened by the immaterial of our existence that
holds us under this little light in the bar;

the unplugged microphone, the abandoned stage, the lacklustre city
walls and streets and buildings that discourage the congregation
of poets' Imagination, of Creation, of Illumination, of Poetry, of
Divine Inspiration—

How many will come tonight? Ten? Eleven? Twenty?

Or are they too occupied by memes, GIFs, and Facebook, Instagram
Likes?

who live off the Internet, by the Internet, for the Internet more than
in real life?

who bang their heads and worship mumble rappers who talk about
drugs, sex and money, and drugs, sex and money?

who watch metacommentaries where Youtubers react to other Youtube
videos reacting to other Youtube videos?

who glorify toxic youtubers and their CS:GO teabags, their "fuck you"s,
"pussy"s, "cunt"s and catcalls, booty calls, pranks and legalise "n****"s
because there is no accountability in games and making offensive,
sexist, racist public profile names?

who idolise these toxic Youtubers and become toxic Youtubers themselves?

who dream of quick fame and money by screwing gold mold to their
teeth and sticking pencils up their noses, flashing their boobs, twerking
their butts, selling their virginities 'cause "Catch me outside, how
'bout dat?"

who recite the lmaos, the lols, the xDs, Deez Nuts, the wtfs, the tmrs,
the yolos and woke—woke motherf*****s! Smoke weed 420,
only wear designer, poppin' on X, got a new car, got a new bitch
and I got a new deal, cuz I fuck a bitch and forgot her name,
Gucci Gang, Esskeetit—don't you have enough cocaine?

Oh, Allen, who could have prophesied that drugs have come so far
  as to degenerate a young, healthy mind and overthrow the severe
  effects of cigarettes and alcohol consumption?
That the ritual of taking drugs, is not for the sake of Enlightenment,
  but for the sake of looking cool and dope, chasing the junkie fish
  upstream?

I see the troubles of our Time, the polluted rivers by sweatshop factories,
  the cross-oceanic dumps and rising temperatures of global ignorance
  and selfishness:
of human relations erased and complicated by the easy access of technology;
of Culture monopolised by the obsessions of popular trends and
  materialistic values;
of Literature overshadowed by algorithmic sitcom dramas and sponsored
  free console games;
of News debunked by Twitter tweets and self-proclaimed political
  commentators;
of Zen and reading rituals replaced by TikTok and cheap comedic
  entertainment;
of holy realms of Islam, Christianity, Buddhism, Judaism, Hinduism
  and other spiritual –isms visualised by Pixels, DPI, Consumerism
  and Violence in games for stress relief;
of Imagination, of Creation, of Illumination, of Poetry, of Divine Inspiration
  autonomised by computer randomisation, customisation and a
  simple Command Key of Copy and Paste—
The Future! However dyslexic and disconnected it might seem to be,
  it has its perks:
from Convenience to Diversity to Sufficiency to the breezy air conditioners
  at home; we live in it and cannot live without.
Whether it resides in the fourth dimension or fifth, it exists, when it is
  to others, supernatural, berserk, an out-of-world experience which
  is incomprehensible to the human eye in plural;

we do not belong, as they do not belong to ours.

While there also exists a collective lineage of that of what of where so
    anxiously determined by blood, by memory and by history,

we all succumb to the linear language of existence, unable to comprehend
    what is more than itself and beyond itself: because Time, by itself,
    runs clockwise, never in reverse, and we cannot turn back time…
    So I say,

Let there be light! Let there be wine! Let there be endless supply
    of liquor and happy hours till nine! Let there be murmurs! Let
    there be talks! Let there be overflowing conversations among
    poets who reconvene in the twilight hours before the session
    starts! Before the tall tables are piled up with pints and glasses
    and bottles of Clarity and Inspiration! Before the mic reclaims
    its authorial presence in the brilliant spotlight of the stage, its
    polyglottic voice of empowerment passing from one speaker to
    another to Enlightenment! Let there be everlasting Poetry! Let
    there be Joy and Sorrow and Anger and Frustration and always,
    Forgiveness! Let there be Nostalgia! Let there be Innocence! Let
    there be Resonance of the Soul! Let there be celebrations of the
    Ephemeral! Let there be appreciations of the Eternal and the Eternal
    Poets of the Past and Present! Let there be poets and brave poets of
    our Time!

Because within this bar of sentimental lights, there are the Peel Street
    Poets.

Henrik Hoeg, Jason Lee, Andrew Barker, Akin Jeje, Victoria Walvis,
    Vish Nanda, Paola Caronni, Blair Reeve, Jesamine Dyus, Nishanth
    Krishnan, Peter Kennedy, Daniel Hamilton, Sam Powley, Trevett
    Allen, Stefania Albanese, Liam 666, Cecil Calsas, Nashua and Angus
    Gallagher, and many many more—

we have our Shakespeares, our Yeats, our Plaths, our Beats, our Angelous,
    our Peels;

poets who guard the morals of Time and Beauty in timeless craft,
and hold their hearts upon the line, a mild schizophrenic sapience purl
    in every syllabic stop.
Let there be light! Let there be good and precious Poetry tonight!
Oh, Peel Street Poets of our Time, when will we march out of the wet
    sewer alley of Stanley Street and crowd Cochrane, Wyndham and
    Aberdeen with Poetry and claim the whole of Peel Street ours?

Acknowledgements

I would like to express my deepest appreciation to the brilliant poets of Peel Street Poetry, old and new. They have witnessed my transformation as a writer over the years. They are playful, lively and an inspiration to my work: Henrik Hoeg, Jason Lee, Andrew Barker, Akin Jeje, Victoria Walvis, Vish Nanda, Paola Caronni, Blair Reeve, Jesamine Dyus, Nishanth Krishnan, Peter Kennedy, Daniel Hamilton, Sam Powley, Trevett Allen, Stefania Albanese, Liam 666, Cecil Calsas, Nashua and Angus Gallagher and many more.

I couldn't have made it through the past few tough years of pursuing my literary ambition while taking up a job without the people who showed support. My fellow MFA writers from the University of Hong Kong have been keeping the writers circle alive: Jenny Chang, Christina Matula-Hakli, Shivani Salil Shinde, Hong Lee Chan Kelly, Mariella Candela, Gabrielle Tsui, Christy Hirai and Fung Ying Cheng.

Robert Burton and Lenore Look, you are more than just colleagues—you're my literary mentors. Eric Leung and Matt Huang, your support has been a great encouragement to me.

To my PGDP classmates, I feel honoured to have crossed paths with you in our chapter to become teachers: Vivian Cheng, Heidi Chan, Tsz Shun Lo Bernard, Jerry Pang, Sabrina Chan, Pansy Ng, Manman Chan, Lynn Cheng, Chloe Chi, Cyrus Kwan, Hebe Lai, Sybil Lam, Jessie Lee, Miki Lo, Angela Siu, Angie Tam, Twinkle Tam, Niki Tung, Alfred Wu, Michelle Yang and Janet Yuen.

My dearest friends, Chris Ng, Richard Yeung and Tony Lam, you're like brothers since day one. Thank you all for being my constant pillars in life. Sidrah Khan, thank you for accompanying me in the worst of times.

To the talented team of editors at Atmosphere Press who have worked so closely with me in the past few months to get my poetry collection in view of the public eye: Alex Kale, Trista Edwards, Ronaldo Alves, Kyle McCord, Erin Larson-Burnett, Cassandra Felten, and Cameron Finch.

To my mother, who has been so patient with me. Thank you for supporting me all these years and for the stories that inspired my poems.

Finally, to my partner-in-crime, Zabrina Lo, for the beautiful cover art and for standing by me as I take on the difficult path to be a writer in Hong Kong.

About Atmosphere Press

Atmosphere Press is an independent, full-service publisher for excellent books in all genres and for all audiences. Learn more about what we do at atmospherepress.com.

We encourage you to check out some of Atmosphere's latest releases, which are available at Amazon.com and via order from your local bookstore:

Melody in Exile, by S.T. Grant

Covenant, by Kate Carter

Near Scattered Praise Lies Our Substantial Endeavor, by Ron Penoyer

Weightless, Woven Words, by Umar Siddiqui

Journeying: Flying, Family, Foraging, by Nicholas Ranson

Lexicon of the Body, by DM Wallace

Controlling Chaos, by Michael Estabrook

Almost a Memoir, by M.C. Rydel

Throwing the Bones, by Caitlin Jackson

Like Fire and Ice, by Eli

Sway, by Tricia Johnson

A Patient Hunger, by Skip Renker

Lies of an Indispensable Nation: Poems About the American Invasions of Iraq and Afghanistan, by Lilvia Soto

The Carcass Undressed, by Linda Eguiliz

Poems That Wrote Me, by Karissa Whitson

Gnostic Triptych, by Elder Gideon

For the Moment, by Charnjit Gill

Battle Cry, by Jennifer Sara Widelitz

I woke up to words today, by Daniella Deutsch

Never Enough, by William Guest

Second Adolescence, by Joe Rolnicki

About the Author

Tom K.E. Chan holds an MFA in Creative Writing at the University of Hong Kong, where he also holds his BA in Language and Communication. He is a poet for PoetryOutLoud Hong Kong and Peel Street Poetry. His poetry chapbook is published in Earthbound Press Poetry Series (Vo.2, No.7) . His other poems have also been published in Proverse Hong Kong, Peel Street Poetry, 聲韻詩刊 Voice & Verse Poetry Magazine, HK Vanities and Cha: An Asian Literary Journal. His short story, The Battle of the Masks, is published in Hong Kong Writers Circle's 17th Anthology, *After the Storm*.

www.ingramcontent.com/pod-product-compliance
Lightning Source LLC
Chambersburg PA
CBHW031339060726
47590CB00007B/2534